Face of Courage

RISE FROM THE RUBBLE

JOSEPH M. CAMMARATA

authorHOUSE®

AuthorHouse™
1663 Liberty Drive
Bloomington, IN 47403
www.authorhouse.com
Phone: 1-800-839-8640

First published by AuthorHouse 7/1/2010

ISBN: 978-1-4520-0256-9 (e)
ISBN: 978-1-4520-0254-5 (sc)
ISBN: 978-1-4520-0255-2 (hc)

Library of Congress Control Number: 2010905721

Printed in the United States of America
Bloomington, Indiana

This book is printed on acid-free paper.

Special Thanks

First and foremost, I want to thank God for the sacrifices you made to make me the person I have become.

I want to thank my blood brother, my hero, Michael F. Cammarata, for being the greatest inspiration in my life. You are forever missed. I love you. Until we meet again.

Special thanks to my mother, Linda, who is no longer with us. You were the strength in my life since birth. I love you with all my heart, and you truly are my hero.

To my wife, Stephanie, you are my soul mate, the rock in my life, the mother of my amazing baby girl, Francesca.

To my baby girl, thank you for being beautiful and for having a piece of Uncle Mikey and Nana in you. I love you, my little baby.

I want to thank my father, Joseph M. Cammarata Sr. You have given me an opportunity in life that has helped mold me into the person I am today. I love you, pal.

I want to thank my sister, Kim. Our relationship has gotten stronger over the past few years. I love you.

To my goddaughter, Christina Michael Prince (Nina), I will always be there for you. I love you.

To Nanny Josephine Warren, thank you for being my biggest supporter, I love you.

My cousins Gregory and Lucy Bartocci, and my little cousins, Gregory, Raquel, Toniann, and Sarah, thank you for sticking by me and supporting me.

My cousins John and Sherie Bartocci, and little cousins John and Vincent, I love you guys.

Thank you Uncle Doug and Aunt Josie for passing badge number 1138 to Michael after thirty-three years of service. He, then I, were both privileged to wear it and carry on the family legacy in the fire department.

Great appreciation and thanks to my Aunt Carol and Uncle Nicky for becoming close with us again. To my cousins Jane, Nicky, Nicole Carolyn, Frank, and my baby cousins, Nicholas, Anthony, Frankie, and Valentina, I love you guys and am glad we all have come together once again.

To my family in Long Island, NY, Uncle Jimmy, Aunt Marie, cousins Jimmy boy, and Christine, thank you, I love you all.

Dr. James Warren and Pam Warren, my aunt and uncle, thank you for being there for my mother through her time of need.

To all my family overseas in Austria, I love you all and will see you soon.

To Jennifer Menduina Friscia, thank you for continuing to be part of our family, I will forever honor Mike's request and will always be here if you need me.

To Robert and Genie Annunziato, Frank Campagna, Gary Elder, and all the members of FDNY's Engine Company 28 and Ladder Company 11. Your continued support will forever be appreciated. Thank you. You are our extended family.

To Pete, Fran, Gregory, John, Claudine, Gabrielle, Jade, Kathleen, Nicole, you guys have supported me and have welcomed me into your family. Thank you so much.

I want to thank Maria Michele Anne DeCarlo. You have contributed to the Firefighter Michael Cammarata Foundation, the street renaming, and molding me into the person I became after the eleventh.

Tremendous thanks to Mayor Rudolph Giuliani for the support and sincerity you have shown me. You are a true hero to me.

To Mary Sansone of the Ciao organization, your relentless hard work and ambition have taught me life lessons that I will continue to use as I strive to serve the community.

To Celia Iervasi, your support is so appreciated. You believed in me through thick and thin. You have been a second mother to me, and for that, I am grateful.

Thank you to Dan Meyer, PhD. You have come into my life over the past two years and have helped guide me in a positive direction. For that I am so grateful.

Thank you to the entire Barone family: Frank, Liza, Francesco, Dante, Lorenzo, and Mateo. Your sacrifices to lend Frank to me for support is greatly appreciated.

To Master Barone, a coach for me in my journey through life, a friend, mentor, and martial arts Sensei, I love you, brother.

To Gennaro Manza, thank you for stepping in as best man on my wedding day. Your presence and speech were so powerful, I will always look to you for support. To Patricia, Gennaro III, and Lucianna, I love you, guys.

To Ronn and Carly Pearson, thank you for believing in me. Ronn, you have been an amazing friend and leader. I will always look up to you; you have been a tremendous voice of reason in my life.

Special thanks to Steven Sciarrino. The countless hours of listening to the content of the book and being a supporter in my life are greatly appreciated. You continue to be a great friend as you have always been for the past twenty-five years. You are a true soldier, marching next to me on the battlefield of life. You are one man who has helped me face terror.

I would Like to thank Wendy Pelligrino, Frank Ariemma, and the entire community who participates in the upkeep of Angels Circle. Our Angel's looking down on you are so proud.

Special thanks to Ceasar Claro of the Staten Island Economical Development Group, and Erik Anderson for your past, present, and future support.

To Jerome Crimi, my police officer partner on the eleventh and a great friend, thank you for being there for me since we met. Our bond is unbreakable!

Thank you, Jessica Whitmore-Crimi for being in my life and asking me to be the godfather of your beautiful son, Lorenzo.

To Lorenzo Crimi, I will forever strive to guide you in life to the best of my ability.

To Chris, Melissa, Isabella and Giavanna Vallone, and Brandon and Vince Carrabba, you guys have been amazing friends who helped me become the person I am today.

To Joseph, Michele, Joseph Jr., Raymond, and baby Mattie Cartigiano, the sacrifices you guys made for the hockey tournament will be remembered by us forever, especially my late mother, Linda.

To all my coworkers over the years at NYPD and FDNY, including Peter Palumbo, Thomas Hunt, Pat Moore, Freddy Martinez, I love you all, thanks for being there for me over the years.

Special thanks to Dennis Van Tine, professional photographer from Staten Island, New York, for contributing his powerful photos to my book.

Special thanks to Laura Bruen Photography of Middletown, New Jersey for capturing our family portrait that we cherish.

To Roy Glover, CEO of Dynamic Web Design, your effort on the cover design, and the website is greatly appreciated.

To Nicola Dicostanza, thank you for being one of the most loyal friends I have ever known.

I want to remember those who are no longer with us: all the civilians who perished on the eleventh, the twenty-three NYC police officers, thirty-four Port Authority officers, one Fire Patrol member, one EMS member, and the 343 NYC firefighters who heroically laid their lives down, my Poppy, Sergeant Major George Warren of the U.S. Army, and Grandma Mary Cammarata.

I will never forget Raymond Cartigiano and Matthew Sciarrino. You have raised great sons; we continue to support each other. Kevin Griswold, Philip Flynn, Paul Steele, and Chris Conrad, you passed in youth but will never be forgotten.

Thank you to everyone not mentioned but who have crossed paths with me, you have all played a part in making me who I am today. I love you all. God bless.

Face of Courage
This is my brother Michael's spare bunker coat

First Responders
Jerome and me at Engine 54 in Midtown

Three Generations of Badge #1138
Michael, Uncle Doug, and me: we all wore badge number 1138

Forward

by Ronn Pearson

It was 8:45 am and the world was safe. Terrorism was a word that the children of America had not yet learned, something that happened far from the shadows cast under flags of stars and stripes. Yet a minute later, the safety blanket of the Western World would be stripped away. And a new generation of Americans would be born together, with open eyes fixed on the smoldering blue skies of the New York City skyline.

The Staten Island Ferry wasn't drifting toward downtown Manhattan that September morning. It was slowly inching closer to hell. Aboard, packed shoulder to shoulder, stood hundreds of rescue workers, firefighters and police officers. Each was about to redefine the words *bravery* and *heroism* forever.

Officer Joseph Cammarata waited on the front deck of the boat. And as the entire world watched the South Tower collapse, he witnessed something completely different. Because in that same tragic second, Michael Cammarata was gone. At 22-years-old, Joe's younger brother would be the youngest firefighter to perish that day.

That afternoon, the names of the missing started trickling in. First a few, then dozens at a time. I remember someone telling me that my friend Michael wasn't coming home and that Joe was on the pile, sifting through the nightmare to find him. I'd later learn from Joe that clawing through the wreckage – lifting steel and concrete and the weight of a solemn nation – would prove to be the easy part. For it was the heavy heart, the emotion and chaos that he'd continue to carry for years, that would crush him to the core. (As it turned out, those buildings took the lives of people that were nowhere near the downtown area that day.) The search for answers, the search for a reason why never stopped until Joe found himself completely numb. Completely empty. Completely alone.

Joe Cammarata was at the bottom. The thought of it strikes pain in me. But somehow, Joe summoned the strength to realize the bottom was a gift – a special place to be. Where some see an end, Joe saw a beginning. It was searching the bottom that allowed him search his soul. To build something completely new—a life filled with love, courage and a relentless commitment to honoring the unique spirit of his lost brother.

This is the story told in *Rise From the Rubble*. The story of one man's remarkable journey to the darkest of emotional places. And his inspiring decision to sever ties with that pain and find the gifts that September 11th gave him. A new wife, a wonderful daughter and a deeper connection to an already strong family. It was the only way he knew to help us all make sense of a completely senseless day.

This is Joe's amazing gift. A gift he gives his family, a gift he gives himself and to my great fortune, a gift he gives his friends. And as this amazing man continues to progress, and chase the things he's set out to achieve, it will be a gift for more and more people in the world around him.

- Ronn Pearson

Chapter 1

Out of Control

Driven, committed, anxious, angry, frustrated, controlling, guilty, traumatized, haunted by flashbacks: my life is out of control. This new lifestyle of mine has drained my soul and altered the person I was over the last two and a half decades. I wouldn't wish it on my worst enemy.

Since the fall of 2001, I have not slept through the night, relentlessly haunted by thoughts of the biggest tragedy this country has ever witnessed. Tossing and turning, cold sweats, and insomnia have become a nightly ritual because of an event that was beyond my control. Visions of the dead, burning rescue vehicles colossal in size, fire trucks with a gross vehicle weight of more than thirty-five thousand pounds crushed like a soda can compacted by a stomping foot. Remnants of bodies littered the streets like trash. Human beings were pushed to the point of making an impossible choice: burn to death by fire, suffocate by thick black smoke, or plunge more than a thousand feet to their death.

Massive fires began to consume surrounding buildings room by room, floor by floor. These buildings, which once stood one hundred stories tall, were reduced to sixty-foot high piles of rubble and debris. They no longer served the purpose of conducting business or acting as symbols of greatness of the city but now served as crushing tombs that claimed the lives of thousands.

A tremendous feeling of helplessness started to overcome my body. I began to experience tunnel vision; everything around me was moving in slow motion. Voices were muffled, not understandable to me. How can this be happening? Where is Michael? Has anyone seen Engine 28, Ladder 11? My life at this moment, that very day, collapsed with the same crippling force as those buildings.

Every breath I took that morning after 0950 hours was thick. It felt like millions of razor blades were entering my lungs, tearing them from the inside out, burning as if they were on fire. Foreign substances have been inhaled; what will the aftereffects be? I don't have a mask; I don't care right now. I wanted to help people, and I wanted to find Michael.

I distinctly remember scanning the area around the wreckage, searching for someone, something, that needed immediate attention. But all I remember is being plagued by the sound of hundreds of firefighters' pass alarms—emergency sound devices strapped to a firefighter's air supply—roaring with distress signals. They go off if a firefighter manually triggers them or if they remain motionless for more than one minute. Some were muffled by the wreckage that trapped these men. I remember thinking these alarms signified a trapped or dead rescue worker, hundreds of them. Who was going to save them?

I'd been a cop for a little more than two years. Recently off probation, my rigorous training from the academy was fresh in my mind, but all the training in the world would never prepare you for this. Our supervisors, sergeants, even the commissioner were scrambling, trying to gather as much information as possible to get a better understanding of what to do. I was terrified and received no guidance from superiors; it was a free-for-all. This was out of everyone's control.

After all, the main reasons someone becomes a first responder for the police or fire department is to assess and then take control of a situation and provide an immediate solution to any problem. Firefighters arrive at a fire that may be roaring on the eightieth floor of a high-rise building and, within minutes, have the fire under control. Police officers arrive in many similar chaotic situations—anything from assault, to robbery, or a man with a gun—and quickly exercise their goal: taking control. That early morning in the fall of 2001, the goal of each and every rescue worker was severely compromised. The feeling of helplessness hit each and every one of us.

This was just the beginning. The days that followed were filled with hope, anxiousness, anger, and grief. I possibly witnessed the death of my brother and was now watching bits and pieces of my parents die by the moment. Once again, I was in a position where I could render no aid to my family, the ones I loved. This tore out my heart.

As the minutes went by and we heard no news, the anger started to manifest within my core. My fiancée at the time, Maria DeCarlo, was at my side through the beginning of this catastrophe, but I soon would lose control of this.

In the days after Michael was confirmed missing, the word spread that he was a probie, on the job only a few weeks, the youngest firefighter to become missing that day; he was only twenty-two years old. This sparked media frenzy. Network newscasters swarmed our home. I felt obligated to tell them about Michael, answer their questions, and keep his name alive. Was I doing this to occupy my time? Was I becoming a coward, unable to face the grim reality that was unfolding?

Months after the tragedy, I decided I would prove I still could control big events in my life. My fiancée and I were scheduled to be married in August of 2002. I sat her down and asked her if she would consider moving the wedding up by four or five months. My reasoning for this was that I wanted to provide my family with a piece of happiness in this chaotic time.

From this point forward, I became obsessed with maintaining control. This would soon start chipping away at my relationship with Maria. The marriage would slowly be overcome by the demons of the tragedy. I was once again being controlled by the events of that horrific day. Constant visions of Michael being trapped, suffering, all alone and terrified became etched in my mind.

I became short-tempered. I found myself constantly fighting with my new wife; we were supposed to be happy. I lashed out at the ones who supported me, the ones who loved me. What the hell was going on? I wanted my old life back; I wanted my best friend back. I just wanted to bring him home, and I couldn't. It wasn't possible.

Many people believe that time heals all wounds. I don't think there's a Band-Aid big enough in this world to cover my wounds. Months went by, and the pain seemed to become so intense that I would lie in bed at night feeling short of breath. It seemed as though there were hundreds of pounds of pressure on my chest, constricting my airway. I felt I should probably seek help, as this was affecting me physically now.

Maria reached out to various counselors to obtain help for me. I was tremendously resistant to the methods these counselors tried to exercise to help me. I walked the earth, feeling no one or nothing could help me. How could these unaffected counselors read into my life, analyze my emotions, and provide a remedy for my problem? Were they fucking kidding me? I tried all types of therapists—males, females, young, and old. I felt not one of them had a fucking clue what I was going through! From time to time, I flirted with the idea of telling them, "If you really want to help me, let's go down to the site and look for my brother. He is missing." The idea of therapy was quickly discarded.

Night after night, the insomnia dominated me. The same haunting visions and flashbacks became involuntary movements within my brain, just as one's heart beats or eyes blink. There was no stopping this; there had to be a reason God was doing this to me.

I was unfocused. I was now working at my new career. When I was fulfilling my daily work duties, I would have chills throughout my body, envisioning what Michael may have seen or thought that early morning in the fall of 2001. Will I make it out of this alive, or will I have the same fate as Mike? When I was at work, I was not focusing on what was going on around me but on the raging chaos that was going on in my life. This wasn't fair to me or my family. Someone could have gotten hurt or killed; I was compromising other people's safety because I couldn't control my emotions or the flashbacks. My thoughts confused me: *Will I ever be able to regain control?* Or would my mind forever play author to the chapter you are reading now?

Believe it or not, I started doing well for myself financially. I had no living expenses because I was living in an apartment in my family's home. This enabled me to spend money recklessly. I began to believe I could be happy showering myself with lavish things. I was twenty-five years old and living the single life. I owned three cars: a 2003 Hummer H2, 2003 Jeep Wrangler Rubicon, and an 04 Audi S4. One hundred and forty thousand dollars' worth of cars parked in the driveway, and I still wasn't satisfied.

It didn't stop there. I flew down to Miami, Florida, to step out of the life I was living in New York. I had a great time; I wanted to make this experience part of my everyday lifestyle. I became extremely resourceful in my efforts to convince my father to buy a condo in an upscale area in Miami. This opened the floodgates for me spending tremendous amounts of money. I became addicted to spending money. Whether it was spending hundreds if not thousands of dollars a night in different bars and clubs, I was clearing out the inventory in some of Miami's most exquisite retail stores. I bought a wardrobe that paralleled that of those who lived on Star Island next to South Beach Miami.

I would have paid any price for a moment of happiness. People who were close to me could have associated my actions as those that were addicted to heroin. I was spending hundreds of dollars for a quick fix of happiness.

It didn't stop there: with money comes women. I quickly became addicted to spending time with many women. I was going through women like I would go through clothes in my closet, wearing the outfit once, never twice, and then storing it back in my closet to collect dust—as I did with women's phone numbers.

My behavior as a result of my past was now affecting the lives of everyone close to me. Strangers, friends, and family relationships were falling apart around me. I didn't trust anyone. Childhood relationships that had been in existence for more than twenty-five years were falling apart. My anger radiated to anyone in close proximity to me, like the radiation spewed from an atomic bomb. If the words I spoke to people didn't immediately terminate the friendships, the lingering effects of what I said would later seep into their heads and destroy the friendships.

Jealousy started to consume whatever was left of my soul, corrupting my thoughts and decision-making abilities. After all the shit I was going through, my friends were now going to turn their backs on me? Fuck them, I didn't need them. I was tough as nails. What the fuck was going on? The very foundation of my life left was being demolished right from under me. This wasn't fair to me or anyone else. I needed to get hold of this before someone got hurt. This wasn't the person I was brought up to be.

Could anyone help me? Would I reconcile these damaged relationships? Was there anybody out there who had the answers I was looking for? Help me; the pain was close to unbearable. Should I face it? Or avoid it? My life felt as though I was running on a treadmill and getting nowhere.

Chapter 2

Preparing for a Dream

Let's face it: it is every child's dream to be a police officer or firefighter. Most children are fascinated by superheroes. Whether it's Batman, Spiderman, Superman, or Captain America, we all, at some point in our life, aspired to be just like these characters. We would look up to them as if they were role models within a fictional society. The fascination for me was not the outfits they wore or their powers or weaknesses but their ability to respond to the scene when people needed them most. After all, the superheroes were civilians by day and heroes by night. Superman was Clark Kent, a news reporter. When trouble emerged, he found a phone booth and changed into Superman; he then would fight to save the day. Batman was Bruce Wayne, a rich businessman who wanted to protect the people of Gotham City. When chaos unfolded, he would slide down a brass pole, suit up, and get into his Bat mobile to respond for the betterment of Gotham. Are they any different than police officers or firefighters?

As time went on, Mike and I aspired to be like these heroes in a realistic world. Police officers and firefighters had duties that resembled those of the superheroes we looked up to. Our dream intensified as we became young men. As teenagers, we often spoke about becoming firefighters. We would count down the time as it went by, knowing that eventually we would be required to take a test. We would have to prove ourselves scholastically, mentally, and physically if we wanted our dream to become a reality. The competition would be intense; historically between thirty and thirty-five thousand applicants would compete for a few hundred spots.

In 1997, the first civil service test we qualified to take was the NYC police officer's exam. We seized the opportunity to take this exam. Although we dreamed of being NYC firefighters, our passion lay in helping people and making a difference in society, the same as our father and childhood role models. This was our first opportunity to be part of something tremendous.

We studied several months for the written exam. Within a few weeks, the results were out. We scored well enough to be called for the physical portion of the exam within the next three months. After scoring a perfect score on the physical, we were pushed to the top of the list to be called as NYC police officers. The only thing holding us back was our age. To become a sworn officer of the law, you had to be at least twenty-two. I was twenty years old, and Michael was nineteen. It was now a waiting game.

Day by day, week by week, we checked the *Chief* newspaper, anxiously awaiting the city to release a new firefighter's exam. The last exam had been exhausted; there was now a freeze on hiring. One day, Mike came home with the *Chief* and a huge grin on his face. He slammed the paper down on our kitchen countertop and said, "It's showtime, pal. Test number 7029 will be given in four months!" I responded, "It's now or never. We have to do this; we've waited our whole lives for this."

We had repeated conversations about how we would prepare ourselves. This test was no walk in the park. We began running three to four times weekly to get our cardiovascular condition pristine. When we weren't running, we were training in the gym, utilizing fitness techniques to build muscular endurance, a necessity if you wanted to be a firefighter.

We also wanted to become mentally fit for the written examination. The *Chief* anticipated that roughly sixty thousand people were aligning themselves to take this exam, the most ever for this test. It's a great job, and a lot of great people were competing for only a few hundred spots. We needed a competitive edge.

We got wind of a written course that was going to be given at Labetti Post in our hometown of Staten Island, New York. We eagerly joined the program because we knew every single point on the written examination counted. One single point can mean the difference between being called or having more than a thousand candidates being called before you for a spot in the biggest, best fire department in the world. We wanted this badly; we couldn't let our dream slip away.

Twice a week for twelve weeks, we rigorously trained in an intense classroom environment. In class, we were given tools and techniques necessary to ace this test. We now had to use these tactics instilled in us during about twenty-five hours a week of class time the other five days a week. We never missed a class, a lesson, or a sentence that our course instructors recited. We paid attention to detail in every aspect necessary to achieve greatness. The feeling was intense. There were hundreds of applicants in the classroom competing for one thing: to become one of New York's *bravest*. It may have been a job they were fighting for, but for Mike and me, we were fighting for our dream. No one or nothing was going to stand in our way.

Countless nights before the test, we couldn't sleep. Mike would knock on my bedroom door after midnight on several occasions to see if I was awake. If I was, he suggested we take the books out and drill. I don't think we slept one wink the night before the test. Even though our test site was New Dorp High School on Staten Island, and the test was scheduled for nine o'clock in the morning, we were out the door at half past six. We arrived at the test site about two hours early to review in the parking lot.

At half past eight, the school opened the doors so the test takers could enter the facility. Our hearts were in our throats. We knew every damn question counted, and we hoped we would both ace it, but what if one of us didn't? What would happen then? We knew if we had a bad day, this could mean the difference between achieving a dream and living with the nightmare of not making it for the rest of our lives. The pressure was enormous.

Before we entered our assigned classrooms, we looked at each other, hugged, and said, "Let's do this; let's take what's ours." At this point, chills ran up my spine, I remember taking my assigned seat, clutching my razor sharp number two pencils, and not being able to feel my legs.

The proctor, with the voice of a chain-smoking fiend, told us not to open the test booklet until nine thirty, after she gave us the word to do so. She instructed us there would be no intermissions during the test. Anyone caught cheating would be escorted out of the building, with his or her chances of being a firefighter terminated. When time runs out the test will be over, and she will instruct us to put down our number-two pencils. Anyone who violates these guidelines will be dealt with accordingly. I just wanted her to give us the fucking test; the suspense was killing me. I felt like telling her, "Lady, we wanted this our whole lives, we are not going to fuck this up. Pass out the goddamn test already."

"Begin. Open up your test booklets; you have three hours." I still hear her voice in my flashbacks, as if she herself were the grim reaper. This was the test that changed our lives forever.

To add more fuel to the fire, Mike and I were in the same classroom, sweating like animals. It was a summer day, humid as a tropical rain forest, no air-conditioning. I remember our arms sticking to the desk; it got quite annoying every time we went to bubble in another answer. *We'd better get used to the heat if we want to be firefighters*, I thought.

About a third of the way through the test, I heard Michael sigh. He put his arms up in the air as if he were stretching, and he then put his hand on his forehead and started shaking his head. At this point, I had knots in my stomach. Was he having a hard time? Was he going to make it? *Oh shit, am I going to make it? I feel sick. I have to get through this; I have been waiting for this moment my entire life.*

The instructor posted the time; she announced that we had fifteen minutes left to finish our test. In our training course, we referred to this as the fifteen-minute warning. Our instructors told us we should have been through all the questions by this time and to use this last fifteen minutes to review the challenging questions that may have tripped us up. I looked up; Mike was frantically going through the pages, as was I.

"One minute left."

Shit, I'd better hurry. Mike is hurrying, as I am. I hope he made it.

"Okay, applicants, pencils down."

I put down my pencil and looked over to Mike to get his reaction to the test. I noticed him feverishly erasing an answer.

"I said pencils down now," she yelled at Mike.

Oh shit, is she going to confiscate his paper?

He bubbled in an answer and said, "I'm sorry. I was in a zone; I didn't hear you."

She responded, "I understand you're under pressure, but part of being a firefighter is focusing. Give me your paper. What's your name?"

He told her, "Michael Cammarata."

She said, "Good luck with your test results. I hope I don't read about you one day."

We got in the car and I asked him, "What the fuck is wrong with you, you could have blown it all?"

He said, "Relax, pal, it's over. I think she liked me. She gave me the eyes. She probably asked me my name because she wants to look up my number. Relax."

When we got home, we looked at our answer logs. These were official papers that the city let you leave the facility with, so you can manually check your answers when the next *Chief* came out. The anticipation was running high. Neither of us were patient enough to wait for the *Chief*. We compared our answers verbally, as we excitedly yelled them out. We had all the same answers until we got to question thirty-four, and I said B. He said, "Ehhhhhhhh, I put C. That's the one I crossed out and changed. Look, I originally had B, like you, Joe, but it has to be the wrong answer." We went through the rest of the questions, and our answers were identical. I told him, "I guess we are going to have to wait for the *Chief* to come out to see who is right on question thirty-four." Otherwise, it was a good sign that our answers had been consistent.

A lifelong friend of my father's, Frankie Abruzzesse, told us that his brother Michael, already a NYC firefighter, was setting up a training camp for the physical. We wanted all the details. We needed to score perfect on the physical if we want to achieve our dream.

We arrived at the training facility at 6:00 AM on a Sunday in June, out in Deer Park, Long Island. We were shocked to see it was in the rear entrance of an old warehouse. As we crossed the threshold of the entrance, we were greeted by an overwhelming stench, that of a sweaty, humid boxing gym, something you would see in an old *Rocky* movie. The heat we walked into was unbearable. Mike looked at me and said, "I hope this guy isn't cheap and bumps up the A/C. We can't train in this; we would die." I recall feeling as if I had entered an underground world, perhaps one that was used to conduct illegal dog fighting. My initial reactions about this place were grim.

Between thirty and forty other people were mustering up in small congregations, all trying to figure out the same things as Mike and I: *What the hell are all these contraptions? And what the hell is going to happen to us today?* The contraptions resembled ancient torture devices.

The trainers blew their whistles. "Attention, people. We are not your friends, we don't care that it is 109 degrees in here, but what we do care about is turning you guys into fine-tuned applicants who can endure the Superman test. It's referred to this way because it's the hardest civil service test in the world; men have actually died taking this. We, as instructors, are here to condition you in an extreme environment, to test the fiber of you souls, to have you make the necessary sacrifices to be worthy of occupying a seat at the Rock, AKA Probie school."

The first run through the twelve events I barely made it. I had to stop and vomit in the trashcan. Mike, on the other hand, completed it. Although he was exhausted, he had an edge on his older brother. I felt humiliated that I hadn't make it through unscathed. The Superman test got the better of me; it wasn't until then I felt the kryptonite had set in.

The following weeks tested our drive, commitment, and dedication. Giving up partying on Saturday nights in the summer, waking up every Sunday morning at five o'clock to trek sixty miles to be tortured mentally and physically actually became a top priority as the weeks went on.

As we got closer to the last sessions, our conditioning for the physical became amazing. Mike and I found ourselves completing the course with the same times. Even though Mike may have been less winded, I was now giving him a run for his money. We were both ready to face and destroy the Superman exam on test day.

Although we were nervous the morning of the physical exam, we had a heightened level of confidence that did not have on the written exam. We methodically tackled the test that morning; we finished the events with copious amounts of time to spare. I remember leaving the test site, high-fiving my brother, when a chief in full uniform stopped us and said, "You're brothers, right? Thank you for coming prepared. You guys are what we are looking for on this job."

Driving home, filled with excitement and the radio blasting, we celebrated as if we were children who had just been told that we were going to be the next Captain America. We were one step closer to changing our lives forever. The only things we needed were our list numbers to see where we stood.

Four weeks later, the list numbers were published in the *Chief* for test #7029. M. Cammarata: 105 written, 100 physical, List no. 345. J. Cammarata: 103.5 written, 100 physical, List no. 1298. Holy shit, he beat me by one question.

He laughed and said, "I told you so. I knew when I got yelled at in that class it was worth it. I changed my answer, and it paid off. Hey everyone, I did better than Joe." He immediately started calling me his junior guy, that he had more seniority than me, and that it was only a matter of time before he would be on the battlefield giving me orders.

One question, and he was almost one thousand candidates ahead of me. We surely weren't going to be in the probie class. A typical class had roughly 115 probies in it. Mathematically, one question possibly landed me ten classes behind him. He really was never going to let me live this down. I was fucked.

After the physical exam for the fire department, the police department reached out to me to schedule the psychological component part of the testing. First a seven hundred-question written test and then, based on your answers, an interview with a psychologist. The theory we applicants had was that if you were in the office with the psychologist more than ten minutes, it was problematic, and you probably would go on psychological review, hindering the chances of getting the job. The suspense leading up to the results was nerve-racking.

Thankfully, the psychologist only had two questions for me. He cleared me within three minutes, and the feeling of relief was immeasurable. I was one step closer to becoming a public servant.

Once again, I found myself waiting. The class was scheduled to be sworn in on July 7, 1999. The only problem with this was that I still did not qualify; I would not be twenty-two until July 11. The class was starting without me, and I was devastated. What could be done to get me into this class? I wanted this extremely bad.

Every day that led up to the seventh of July was filled with anxiety and disappointment. I could not believe that my age, short of the cutoff by only four days, was standing in the way of one of my dreams. This was devastating news. On July 11,1999, my birthday, I remember feeling down in the dumps, not enjoying myself at all. The only thing I wanted for my birthday was for my dream to be fulfilled, and it didn't happen.

On July 13, 1999, my mother, Linda, bedridden with breast cancer, answered the phone around seven o'clock. I remember her yelling to me in an exhausted, sickly tone to pick up the phone. The minute I picked up, a man introduced himself as Sergeant so–and-so from candidate screening. Immediately I knew what this was about. He told me to report for duty at the Police Academy at 0630 hours on July 15. I would be sworn in as an officer of the department and start the academy one week after everyone else. I was shocked; the feeling was awesome, and I couldn't believe they called me.

The first day of the academy was awkward. I didn't have my recruit uniform yet, so I had to wear a business suit. The other probationary officers were wearing their recruit uniforms, and I stood out like a sore thumb. Aside from this, the feeling of what not to expect from being new to the police academy experience was terrifying. Instructors constantly yelled at recruits in the hallways and disciplined them. I was walking into a real-life paramilitary boot camp. I was now property of the NYPD.

I was assigned to Company 99-37. Within seconds, I recognized a recruit from Staten Island, New York. He actually went to college with me at St John's University. His name was Jerome Crimi Jr. He stood about five foot nine and weighed about 195 pounds. He had a drive in his eyes to be a police officer that mirrored the drive Mike and I had of becoming firefighters. Immediately, we forged a bond that led to everything from studying to carpooling to and from the academy. Neither of us had a clue what the future had in store for us once we became police officers.

Our experience at the academy was grueling. Our day consisted of waking up at 0430 hours, picking each other up at 0500 hours, and commuting to the academy, which was located on east 20th Street in Manhattan. Our torture session ran from 0700 hours until 1600 hours. I'm serious; I really mean torture. We dreaded walking down 20th Street into that building, but every day we did we were one day closer to our goal. Academically, we attended four different classes a day. We also had a rigorous physical training session that was held in a gym that was 105 degrees. The calisthenics and running were treacherous. One of the hardest things about this experience was counting down the days with Jerome. I felt like we were doing a nine-month prison sentence.

My bond with Jerome strengthened on a daily basis. When you spend as much time with each other as we did under these stressful situations, the bond becomes extremely strong. We started to rely on each other, trusting each other with the very fate that lay ahead. I could definitely see myself working side by side with him, possibly giving my life for him.

The dream of becoming a New York City firefighter was temporarily put on hold, but the commitment Mike and I had for executing our goal intensified as the days ticked away. We had prepared and would live our dream.

After I'd been a police officer for about two years, Michael received his letter to report for duty to the Fire Academy on May 2, 2001. On his receipt of his acceptance, the jokes started to flow in my direction again. He referred to himself as the "bravest" and talked about how he would teach me the ropes if I ever got called. He also told me that our Uncle Doug, who was a New York City firefighter from 1960–1993, was going to pass his badge #1138 down to him the day he was to be sworn in. The sentimental value of this act my uncle was performing was monumental. It signified the newly formed family tradition that would continue to be carried on. Although I was envious he was given my uncle's badge, I was truly happy for my brother. I told him congratulations on the next phase toward achieving his dream. He beat me by one question, one goddamn question; I guess he was more prepared for the dream.

NYPD Graduation: Me, Dad, and Mike
Notice him breaking balls with the Dunkin Donuts bag

Chapter 3

Call to Duty

The sun penetrated the venetian blinds that covered the sliding glass door I was sleeping next to; it was the first thing I recall as I opened my eyes. I jumped out of bed, knowing that it was going to be another amazing day from a weather perspective. These types of days provided a comfortable atmosphere for the relaxed life I was living.

I woke next to Maria, my fiancée, around 0730 hours. We both raced to the bathroom to take showers to start our workday.

"Ladies first," she yelled as she slammed the bathroom door and started to run the shower. I put on the TV as I waited my turn to shower. I watched the weather, "Ah, another amazing day," I said to no one. As we were approaching fall, my favorite time of the year, I couldn't help but count the days until the cool weather approached. I always viewed this time of year as a power season for me.

About an hour and a half before my day started, Michael, a probationary firefighter in Ladder Company 11 in Manhattan, was preparing to leave home. My mother hugged him and said, "Mike, be careful." He accepted her hug, told her he would, and told her he loved her.

By the time I was just opening my eyes, Mike had already arrived at the firehouse in Alphabet City in lower Manhattan, relieved firefighter Gary Elder, and assumed the position of Can in the truck. It is customary for members of the fire department to arrive at least one hour earlier than their scheduled shift to relieve another member from duty. A probationary firefighter should be there at least an hour and a half early. This has been a tradition for well more than a hundred years.

Usually I rose about 0630 hours and would go to the gym with my police partner, Jerome Crimi. But today, he had a tour change; instead of a start time of 0930 hours, he was to commence his workday at 0800 hours. This gave me a much needed day of rest from the gym.

It was now 0830 hours. I started my car, rolled down the windows, and started to play a Paul Oakenfold CD, a type of upbeat trance music, exactly what I needed to put me in a zone to start my productive day at work. Listening to this type of music afforded me the opportunity to enter my own world temporarily—well, at least for the entire commute to work. This was my private time, an escape from the world's daily routine.

About sixteen minutes after I left Maria's home at 0846 hours, while driving, oblivious to the worlds unfolding events, little did I know the North Tower of the World Trade Center had been struck by an aircraft. My phone rang. I looked at the time on my radio; it read 0847 hours. It was Maria from work. With a definite urgency in the tone of her voice, she said, "A plane hit the World Trade Center." My initial feeling was relaxed. I responded in the same fashion by telling her, "Oh man, an inexperienced pilot. It must be a small plane. We will probably respond and be there all day." Simultaneously, I received another call coming in to my cell phone; the caller ID read Jerome. I told her I had to go, and I clicked over. "Joe, the fucking Twin Towers just got hit by an airplane. The whole building is on fire. Christina is in there, and she might be dead." "Jerome, let me go. Calm down. I am on my way."

I hung up and switched to 1010 WINS, a NYC AM news radio channel. I wanted to have a good understanding of what I was sure I was going to be responding to once I got to work.

About one minute went by, and the phone rang again; it was Jerome. "Joe, this is crazy. The whole building is on fire; the smoke is insane. I tried calling Christina, but she is not answering. I hope she is okay."

"Jerome, I am about fifteen minutes out. I will see you then. Unlock my locker and lay out my gear. She will be okay, I promise you."

I hung up with him and phoned Maria. "Jerome is panicking; he thinks that the girl he is dating, Christina, is hurt in the incident. She is not answering her cell phone or her work phone."

"I hope not, Joe, this is nuts."

I told her I would keep her posted but had to go.

The initial level of relaxation I had when I first found out about the incident was now getting slightly elevated, as does a thermometer when it is put into heat.

Just about the same time this was happening at 0855 hours, my brother Michael called my father with hopes to reach him but was unsuccessful. He was directed to my father's voicemail and left a gripping message. "Dad, a plane hit the World Trade Center. I am on my way there. I am all right. Tell everyone I love them."

It was two minutes after nine. I just received news via the radio that the South Tower had gotten hit by an airplane. The first light went off in my head: *terrorism*. The phone rang again; I was now dreading every time I heard my phone ring, because I feared what or who was going to be on the other line. "Jerome, what's up?"

"Joe, a second fucking plane hit the other tower. The plane looks like it is hanging out of the building. This is bad, man."

"Jerome, we're under attack. This has to be terrorism. I am about five minutes away, hang tight." A very bad feeling overcame my entire body. I felt like I lost my bearings. I was now hurrying toward my command, selflessly but cautiously passing red lights and large intersections with my four-way flashers on while hitting the horn.

My heart was racing a mile a minute. I found myself nervously using my personal car as if it was an emergency vehicle.

I arrived at my command, which was on the waterfront in Staten Island, located directly across the water from the World Trade Center. It was 0911 hours when I parked my car and started running toward the building. In the distance, I saw Jerome. He was staring lethargically at the catastrophe. I grabbed his arm to wake him from a trance that had been controlling him. "Jerome, Jerome, let's go."

In the tone of a zombie, he said, "Look, look, man." We looked out to the towers in disbelief. Large sections of the buildings were engulfed in flames. The feeling was surreal. Everything was in slow motion for a few seconds. I felt like I had entered a realm of horror I had never been exposed to in my twenty-four years of life.

I ran to the building and ascended five flights of stairs as if I was a cat that had been frightened or traumatized. I busted the locker room door open to find my uniform and gear strategically laid out by Jerome, so I could dress in half the amount of time. I was partially dressed, descending five flights of stairs, still buckling my gun belt. I was jumping down half-flights of stairs. I was racing toward uncertainty, as was Michael, as were all the rescue workers, and we all were doing it with one thing in mind: to help people.

The anxiety really started to build as I exited the lobby and saw the rapidly deteriorating conditions of the towers, as well as the many officers scurrying around to combat-park our emergency vehicles so we could respond quickly.

We were still awaiting orders to proceed to the towers. Because our unit's start time was always 0930 hours, members were still racing into the command to be present for duty. We needed all the manpower for this; this was the big one.

By 0936 hours, just six minutes after our routine start time, our unit was racing lights and sirens toward the Staten Island ferry. Closed to civilians, we knew we were going to commandeer it and head to the towers. This was our best means of unimpeded response.

It was 0945 hours; we now disembarked via the Staten Island side of the ferry and were heading to the island of Manhattan. Occupied solely by rescue personnel, police cars, ambulances, and fire trucks, I am sure all the minds of everyone onboard were occupied with the same thoughts that I had, *Holy shit, this is chaos. Am I going to make it out of this day alive?*

As we were halfway across the bay that separated the two islands, something happened. At first, I couldn't believe my eyes; I thought they were deceiving me. Could my mind be playing tricks on me?

There was a tremendous manifestation of smoke, and then the accelerated cognition kicked in: there was only one tower standing. One had vanished. A powerful, almost crippling feeling hit me and paralyzed my entire body. Michael was working that morning, that moment, the second that building collapsed—so did any chance of survival for Michael. Something intuitively told me he was dead.

As I looked out at the sole twin of a family of buildings that stood as an icon to the entire world, I broke down in tears, feeling as if I had also lost what most people believed to be my identical twin.

Crushing moment

Agony

Disbelief

Pain

Shock

Terror

Captain Bel Castro, the commanding officer of my unit, Staten Island Task Force, ordered the ferryboat captain to stop the ship. He awaited answers from his superiors.

His actions, so he could gain a sense of what to do—although wise—created turmoil on the boat. Members of all the units, including me, were demanding we keep moving. I wanted to know what happened and especially needed to find Mike. His answers didn't come fast enough, but he ordered the ferryboat captain into Manhattan.

I have crossed these waters many times on the ferry, but this time was different. Besides being life changing for all of us, I never realized that a vessel of this size could travel twice as fast as it typically does. We were racing to uncertainty!

It was now 1028 hours. We had just pulled into port on the Manhattan side when, all of a sudden, we were hit with a second wave of smoke and debris. It resembled a major snowstorm. There was zero visibility and complete and total darkness. Officers running from the towers were frantically screaming out on the radio that the second tower had collapsed. I couldn't believe what was happening. *This can't be real.*

As we made our way toward the location where the towers once stood, we were accosted by the ugly existence of death and disaster. We tried to get to the epicenter of the collapse but were stopped several blocks away; debris created roadblocks we couldn't get through. Although eager to rescue and flanked by my partner, Jerome Crimi, we were redirected to a mobilization point under the Williamsburg Bridge on the Manhattan side.

It was 1050 hours when we arrived at the mobilization point. I frantically tried to call home from a payphone because all cell phones in the area were either overloaded with calls or the signal towers had collapsed or malfunctioned. The frustration and helplessness I felt was daunting. It wasn't until 1130 hours that I was able to get through to my mother. She told me she hadn't heard from Mike yet. I assured her he would be okay, calmed her down, hung up, and then was frozen by the chilling feeling of impending doom that controlled the region of my neurological system responsible for motion.

At 1145 hours, our unit followed orders that were given to us via a Level IV citywide mobilization to execute tactfully a painstaking grid search for those injured, dead, or trapped, or for any suspicious activity or packages. We were to clear the area and report back to Citywide Central.

By 1225 hours, we had concluded our search; I couldn't help but think that if Mike was in a two-block radius of the building when it collapsed, he was dead. As I tried to comprehend my thoughts, a male spotted us and asked if the B train was running. Jerome instantaneously took the liberty to respond by saying, "Are you out of your fucking mind, buddy? We are at a heightened state of emergency, the trains are shut down, and you need to walk your ass across the bridge into Brooklyn." Off he went into the dust, as shocked at Jerome's response as he was about what had just happened at the World Trade Center. The whole grid search was fruitless, a waste of manpower and time. I became frustrated with the whole scenario. I wanted to do something, wanted to help people, wanted to find Michael, and I felt like I had my hands tied behind my back.

It was now inching closer to 1300 hours and still no word from Mike. My hope was beginning to fade. Our unit was redirected to Fulton Street and Water Street. *We have to do something, I can't take much more of this!*

We sat there, anxiously awaiting our orders. This was fucking bullshit; my anxiety was reaching the boiling point. I wanted to go to the collapse site and search for Mike. It had been more than six hours since the collapse. I wanted to find answers, and I wanted them now. I felt as if I was trapped clear across the country, helpless and with no means of getting to my city when I was actually mere blocks from the devastation. I could smell the burning and see the looks of terror on civilians' faces. This was the city I'd sworn to protect, and I was ordered to *stand by and wait*. Stand by and wait? Those words fled my brain the second my city was attacked. *This is bullshit.*

I pulled Jerome to the side and told him I wanted to go to the site with him and look for Mike. I told the captain I needed to search for my brother and make sure that he was accounted for. He said, "No way. You're not going up there to look for him. You're my responsibility, and I will not let any of my personnel get hurt!"

Jerome and I feverishly tried to persuade him to let us and two other cops take a police van to canvass the site. He granted my wish.

Ten minutes later, I found myself having a tremendous problem trying to reach the site. The same debris that restricted our access near the ferry was now impeding us in a totally different region.

I opened the door to the van and got out. I started walking on top of some of the debris. My legs were getting stuck in every void on the piles of debris. It seemed impossible to climb over the rubble. When my fellow officers asked me what I was doing, I told them I was going to continue on foot from there. They argued with me and told me I couldn't go alone. They dragged me back into the van, against my will, and drove me back to Fulton and Water.

It was now 1630 hours. The Staten Island Police trustee, Richie Rodriguez, escorted me in full uniform to Mike's firehouse on East 2nd Street in the Alphabet City section of the lower east side of Manhattan, to find out what was going on with Mike. On our arrival, I noticed Engine 28 and the men were back in quarters. Frank Campagna, a probie who came out of the academy to the same firehouse with Mike was there covered in dust. I asked him and Captain Carlin of Engine 28 where Mike was and if he was dead. No one in the firehouse had accountability from the Ladder Company. I fell to my knees, crying in total disbelief. My worst fears were moving closer and closer to becoming a grim reality.

It was now approaching 1700 hours. The seasoned trustee took me back to Fulton and Water, where my unit was still mobilized. I asked the captain if I could have a word with him. We walked to the side, and that's when I told him I needed to head up to the site on foot. I needed to do my own search. "Captain, if it was your brother, you would do the same. I have to go."

He told me flat out, "No, I can't let you possibly go unaccounted for."

With an amazing rage coupled with courage, I told him, "I fucking resign then." I ripped off my shirt, badge, and gun belt and then slammed them to the pavement at his feet with the force of a gladiator. I no longer felt helpless. I began to make my way toward the destruction with the trustee by my side. Jerome started to follow and was ordered by Bel Castro to stop. He told him he would suspend him effective immediately. Jerome pleaded, "Joe is like a brother to me. I want to go." I forced Jerome to stay; I assured him I was strong, and I would be okay.

It was now 1715 hours. I arrived at the site. I stopped and tried to comprehend the magnitude of damage, loss of life, and destruction that occurred here. I momentarily believed I was clairvoyant and knew the outcome for me and my family would be crippling.

I was trekking through sludge of ash and debris that had been flooded with water from broken fire hoses and busted fire hydrants. I scanned the area, trying to see if Michael or any other survivors needed immediate help. Besides firefighters' emergency pass alarms roaring deep beneath the rubble, everything was utterly silent. Groups of freshly mobilized firefighters awaited orders. I ran to several packs of them to see if anyone had seen Ladder 11. They all looked at me like I had six heads. I continued to search with Richie, but I saw a look of grief for me in his eyes.

It was 1730 hours. I had seen what I had believed to be an old-time, retired firefighter walking aimlessly, with a look about him that mirrored death. He reminded me of a ghoul from the Michael Jackson *Thriller* video. I asked him if he thought anyone survived. He looked at me with a grim face, and with a voice that resembled Vincent Price's said, "Anyone who was here where these buildings fell are no longer with us." To this day, I will never forget him or what he said.

I was now directly in front of World Trade Center Building 7. It was fully engulfed in flames; I am talking of at least thirty to thirty-five floors. A firefighter next to me told me, "This ain't good, man, that building is going to come down. We are in a bad place right now."

All of a sudden the ground started to shake like an earthquake. I froze. I looked up, and the building was coming down. I put my head down and started to run. I felt like I was not getting very far. The soaked debris that resembled a white paste or plaster was at least eight inches to a foot deep. I believed I was running in quicksand. Debris was crashing down, and the sound of failing girders and twisted metal overpowered my physical abilities. But I kept running. My conscious asked me, *What if Mike is alive and you die now?* I ran and ran and ran. I wanted to survive for my family. Debris and a cloud of smoke passed me. *Is this how it's going to end?* It sounded like I was in the middle of a racetrack and thirty NASCAR drivers were flying past me. I ran and hooked a left near the clothing store Century 21 and kept running. I didn't stop until I reached a safe area. Exhausted, with visions of what had just happened, I stopped in front of Trinity

Church across the street from the site. I turned around and Richie, the trustee, was not behind me; he was missing.

I ran to a police officer in the street. I told him to give me a radio, that I was a cop who needed to call my unit. He looked at me with disregard. "I don't know who you are, and you are not getting my radio."

With fright and emotion building up inside, I told him, "Give me your fucking radio; I need to call a 10-85," the signal for "officer needs assistance." At that point, I was unsure the reason he handed me the radio, but he did. "10-85, 10-85, another building fell, 10-85 Staten Island Task Force portable unit to Task Force C.O." At this point, Bel Castro sent Jerome as well as two other officers to come get me at my location.

They brought me back to the mobilization point at Fulton and Water. The captain was eagerly awaiting my arrival. Bel Castro reamed me out. He told me I put other officers as well as myself at risk, and that I was a danger to myself as well as the department. He ordered me to go home.

With disgust and torment, I obliged. This was the first time in my career I felt ashamed to be a New York City police officer. I'd wanted to help the people of the city, but my captain kept me cooped up at the mobilization point, allowing critical time to pass. This was disheartening.

The delegate, Mike Guglielmo, escorted me home in the same police van I'd ridden in the day my life changed forever, when I'd originally been called to duty as an officer. The ride off the island of Manhattan was silent.

As we exited the city—and the apocalypse that had happened to Manhattan—I recall seeing the robust smoke vanish as we exited the Brooklyn Battery Tunnel into Brooklyn. Although cloudy with remnants of destruction that blew over the bay, we seemed to be heading into a clear area of refuge. It was closed to the general public but open to rescuers. We approached the Verrazano Bridge and were greeted by the most amazing sunset I have ever seen in my life. One thing that solidified the magnitude of the destruction was the vacancy of vehicular traffic on the bridge. A roadway that easily accommodates a hundred thousand cars a day was as barren as the tundra. This was something that irked me as it was happening.

It was about 1830 hours. We had turned the corner of Mike's and my street, Kingdom Avenue in Staten Island, and slowly drove up the block. Our house was on the farthest extension from Amboy Road, the block we turned down. As we got about midway up the street, it almost looked like the street had major congestion at the end, near my house. As we got closer and the obstruction came into focus, I realized it was about thirty vehicles. The cars, and the fashion they were parked in, looked like a block party was taking place. The delegate dropped me off about a half of a block from my house. I got out and ran between several parked cars. I raced toward my front door and barged in. My clothes and skin covered in thick white dust, I barreled through the occupants in my house, feverishly trying to locate my parents. These people were friends, family, distant family, and acquaintances, all aware of what had happened and that Michael was missing. They were mustered in front of and inside my house to pay respects and keep vigil.

I followed the loud screaming and crying to find my mother deep in the kitchen, crying as my father hugged her. I couldn't believe what was happening. This couldn't be real.

I will never forget that day. My father walked me outside, far away from everyone, looked me in the eye, and with tears in his eyes and the look of disaster on his face, said, "If he doesn't come home tonight, it's just not good, Joe." My whole world collapsed. My hero, the man who was an icon of strength to me, was crippled helplessly right in front of me.

The night dragged on. As every minute passed, the suffering for my family intensified. Several people stayed at the house, trying to assist with the process of officially declaring Michael missing, as well as calling all the hospitals and morgues searching for answers. It was clearly the longest, most horrific day of my life, of all our lives.

I quickly set up multiple phone lines, cell phones, and TVs in our kitchen. It became our hub of communication to the world and our lifeline to finding out about Michael.

That night I had to realize that the days that lay ahead of me would test the fabric of my soul. I would have to be strong for my entire family while we waited for some status on Michael. How was I, or we as a family, going to deal with the thought of not knowing? Was he missing, trapped, or dead? It became a cruel waiting game.

Bring Home Michael

Chapter 4

Premonition

What would you do if you had an eerie feeling you were going to die? Would you tell your family? Would you tell them what you truly felt about them? What course of action would you take to provide comfort to your loved ones if that feeling came to fruition?

A few days after the collapse, my mother ventured into Michael's room, searching for official documents and materials that would help the fire department compile the necessary data to activate their 9-11 database. Searching in his night table next to his bed for his birth certificate and any artifacts that could provide some substantial DNA, she stumbled on a tri-folded piece of white computer paper with what looked to have blue inscribing on it.

As her eyes, filled with their usual tears, slowly came into focus, she was able to read the inscription previously left in blue ink. It was titled,

"If anything was ever to happen to me." She put the letter back in its proper place, hurried out of the room into the hall, and called me. "Joey, Joey, hurry up, come here, Joey come to Mike's room."

I was on the floor above, watching the minute-by-minute recovery updates from Ground Zero in the living room with Maria. I quickly ran down to aid her, as if something horrific had happened. Jumping down the stairs, stumbling, I turned the corner into the hallway that led up to his room. I found her sitting on the floor in tears, hysterical. "Ma, what the hell happened? You okay?"

Her words were almost unrecognizable. For a second, I thought I might need a translator. "He left a letter, and it's in his drawer."

"What? What the hell are you talking about?"

"Joey, just go read it. I can't. It's in the top drawer of his night table, to the left of his bed."

I followed her instructions. The nightstand that she had directed me to was situated below a bone-chilling piece of art. Framed in thick, black outlining, it was a photograph of the NYC skyline, blacked out, as if the entire city had had a massive power outage. The skies were gray, cloudy, and dark; the towers stood vacant, black in color, as if they were the charred remains of what had unfolded.

Impending doom

The only object that preserved its natural color was Lady Liberty, nestled in the choppy waters of the Hudson. She stood out like an icon of freedom and liberty, something that we needed in the days that followed. As I reached into the drawer, I hesitantly grabbed hold of his letter. I read the title of the document. I became paralyzed instantaneously. I was frozen for the moment; I must have read the title three times before I could muster the courage to move forward. I cautiously opened the tri-folded document, knowing that whatever the content was, it would change our lives forever. What could this letter mean? It again was titled at the top of the page. My heart began to race, my hands became clammy, my head was drenched with sweat, my eyes started to fill with tears, and my throat started to close. I was trying to focus so I could absorb the full impact of the content that lay there in my hand. I slowly opened the folded letter.

If anything ever happens to me ...
1. Take care of Jenna
2. Don't mourn as this is the career I chose
3. Make my spirit live on
4. Remember I love you all and will be waiting for you upstairs

Signed (in cursive),
Michael Cammarata Badge #1138

I had the mobility of a statue. I was absolutely still, shocked at the content of the letter. I couldn't fathom what had inspired him to write these last requests. I read it several times, searching for numerical digits that would summarize a date so I could try to piece together when, why, and what led him to write this final testament. But it was not dated.

The discovery of this letter could be compared to when an archaeologist finds an artifact after a significant event in history. An archaeologist painstakingly searches for the time of its creation and for answers to hundreds of questions that arise as a result of its discovery. *But when was this letter written?*

The word of his letter quickly spread within my family with the equivalent magnitude of a five-alarm fire. Burning questions started to mount by the second. Everyone wanted to know when he wrote it and what event had happened in his life that had prompted him to write it.

Taking Care of Jenna
Jennifer and Michael Hugging

Family told friends, friends told their friends, who then told strangers. Within days the news reporters caught wind of the letter and once again were reaching out to us to hear the story behind the letter. Although in a sense it was painful because we didn't know the answers, I felt compelled to speak of him posthumously.

Obligated by his third request, "Make my spirit live on," I took his inscription as an order by a superior. I wanted to follow the commands of a leader turned hero. It became my duty, as his brother and a fellow soldier of that day, to carry out his last wishes from this point forward.

That night I was again plagued with insomnia. I couldn't even force myself to fall asleep. I relentlessly hunted in my head for answers that may never come. I didn't even realize that I was not going to find the answers there but was just spinning my wheels of emotion without getting anywhere. I always viewed wonder as something great. After all, the great philosophers, such as Socrates and Aristotle, thrived on wonder. But since the discovery of the letter, the wonder that was now housed inside my mind was torturing me.

Not only was I searching for Michael or answers about each and every footstep he took on the eleventh, I was also searching for the explanation behind this letter. How many straws would it take to break my back?

As the days passed, I had no answers. My search for an explanation was fruitless. My journey to conquer the truth was as barren and dry as the Sahara. I began to get anxious. I had an unquenchable thirst for finding each and every answer to the questions that arose as a result of this letter.

I thought constantly, *I am a police officer, I am intelligent, I will be as resourceful as possible, and something will give. Someone out there has the answers. I just have to find them, no matter what I have to do.*

Every night I attempted to fall sleep, and every morning I rose I found myself clutching the letter. I studied it until my eyes became blurry. I knew the location of every grain and blemish on both sides of the paper but not the answers behind the letter.

"Take care of Jenna." That an easy one; we love her and will continue to call her family forever. "Don't mourn me as this is the career I chose." This kid must have had a feeling, something must have happened, but if it wasn't an event, what was it? Who or what told him in advance it was going to be his time? It didn't read, "Don't mourn me, because I will die of a heart attack, or get hit by a car, or die in a car accident"! It was specific, to the point, it was as direct as can be, and he had to know. He had to know he was going to die in the line of duty, serving the city. It was a premonition turned reality. It was amazing. The only thing was, it was my kid brother and that was painful.

"Make my spirit live on." This request, who was it for? I didn't really care, I will be the one forever, and I do mean until I perish one day, who will relentlessly carry out this wish. Michael will forever live on through me and the future children who are the offspring of the Cammarata name. Hell, I will even try to make his spirit live on through each and every human being who will listen to me tell his story. As a matter of fact, even if he didn't request this, I would do it anyway.

He was very clever at the end of the letter; he reminded us something monumental. In his last request, he made sure he would comfort us. It's emotional to even put this one on paper: "Remember I love you all and will be waiting for you upstairs." Inspirational yet comforting, it still doesn't bring him back. But I do feel a hell of a lot better knowing that he was convinced he was going upstairs and not downstairs. That's a fucking relief.

The level of maturity that this twenty-two-year-old rookie fire-fighter exhibited to the world is amazing in itself. Some senior members of Engine, 28 Ladder 11, who have been fighting fires more than twenty years, told me they would never have the courage to write a letter like that. They spoke of the type of guts it takes to fight fires, but they said if they had all the guts in the world, they didn't think they would have what it took to put their final requests on paper like that, anonymously.

IF ANYTHING EVER HAPPENS
TO ME.......

1. TAKE CARE OF JENNA
2. DONT MOURN AS THIS IS THE CAREER I
   CHOOSE
3. MAKE MY SPIRIT LIVE ON
4. REMEMBER I LOVE YOU ALL AND W.ll
   BE WAITING FOR YOU UPSTAIRS

Final Requests of a Hero

Mike was a special person. After a few weeks passed, it didn't really surprise me that he'd written this letter. This was the type of person he was. He always seemed to do great things in life. Now it seemed he was carrying his work in death as well.

Number three on the list became a top priority of mine. I was now in the process of constructing a plan, a plan with tremendous longevity, a plan that would fulfill his biggest request to "Make my spirit live on."

Chapter 5

Making His Spirit Live On

It was now time to carry out his requests. Making his spirit live on became an obsession. I would lie in bed night after night, trying to pinpoint the first thing I could do that would exemplify his wishes.

It was October 1, 2001, four days before Michael's memorial service, and it was on this day that I had a definitive plan to carry out the first means of making his spirit live on forever. Armed solely with a photo of Mike in full bunker gear, taken in the academy, I journeyed from my house to see my friend Dave Lopez. It would be his creativity and talent that would bring my vision to reality. A friend and fellow martial artist of the underground fighting art of American Vadha Kempo, I knew I could depend on him to participate in bringing the first honoring of Mike to fruition.

I arrived at his place of business on Sunday morning, typically Dave's day off. He reported to work that day because of the sentimental importance he knew was tied to this event. This day, at this very place, was where I would forever become one with Michael. As I nervously entered his shop, the bells above the door rang when I pushed the door open. They were a constant reminder of the World Trade Center, because their sound resembles that of four sets of five bells, which signify the loss of a firefighter. That very tone is played over and over again in my head like a CD played on repeat mode. It is the little things like the bells that trigger those violent, diabolical memories of the eleventh. I couldn't let it capture my emotions then as I had a mission to complete: phase one of Mike's wishes.

Dave, an accomplished artist, would create a portrait of Michael in the form of a tattoo and forever brand it on my upper back, on the same side as my heart. He set up an easel and carefully placed Michael's 8 × 11 color photo on it. He told me to relax, take a few deep breaths, and trust his freehand talent as he manually brought Michael back to life on my flesh.

Trusting his experience, I was sure he would resurrect the handsome face of my brother that day. "Joe, are you ready?" I answered yes as I sat in a reverse fashion on his tattoo chair. It was now or never. I again found myself and Michael trusting our fate to the hands of someone else, a feeling that led to a life-changing outcome the last time. This time, I felt confident the outcome would once again change my life forever: I would be one with Michael again.

He began, powering up the shiny, electric tattoo mechanism that housed several razor-sharp needles. A vision of Ground Zero was created in my mind by the operating sound of his instrument. The sounds of rescue workers and ironworkers feverishly operating saws and torches resembled the noise that emanated from Dave's power tool. I found myself living a new routine of being sucked back to the site.

As the device pierced my skin, the pain was ripping and burning, almost unbearable from the first second he started. I looked to Michael for inspiration to continue. This new pain I was feeling was nothing compared to what some victims felt that morning. I should be able to do this standing on my head.

About three hours in, he requested that we break for fifteen minutes. He wanted to rest his hands so he could continue to work on the masterpiece without being plagued by fatigue. Even Michelangelo took periodic breaks during his work.

The last forty minutes, the pain was unbearable. I found myself wishing to have a flashback of that day to mask the physical pain that was being inflicted on me. It was torturous, but it would be worth it; I must make his spirit live on. This was the least I could do for him.

The room went silent. All you could hear was the rapid exhalation of my breaths. Dave sprayed a mist of cool substance on the excruciating area of my back where the resurrection was taking place. He wiped it gently. Could this be it, could he be done?

After six hours, Dave helped me over to the mirror. Weathered yet anxious, I took a breath and a sip of water to regain my composure before I would lay my eyes on Michael once again. The moment of truth: I slowly looked over my right shoulder into a crooked mirror affixed to Dave's wall. There he was, from his shoulders, face, and fire helmet with the 11 truck insignia on it; he exhibited tremendous command. He radiated off my back like a beacon of light that could be seen and recognized from miles away.

With "Face of Courage" above his helmet and "In loving memory of Michael" under his bunker coat, this creation from Dave Lopez was perfection; each painstaking detail was magnificent.

It was half past six; my mother had been anxiously awaiting the arrival of Michael. She was waiting at the window when I pulled up to the house. I didn't even get two steps out of the car before I was greeted by her voice, "Let me see him." I tried to explain to her I had strict orders from the artist not to undress the piece for twenty-four hours. I didn't want to risk infection. But the sad look on her face resembled her daily appearance. I had an opportunity right at that minute to bring solace to her and her bleeding heart.

"Okay, I will do it once, and only once. Get the whole family, including Jen, to the house within the hour, and I will show everyone as a family, just for a few minutes."

About forty-five anxious minutes passed before the unveiling of the work. Everyone was in the living room. I had my shirt off, and my father slowly started to peel off the medical tape that was securing the bandage. "Oh shit, take it easy, it hurts like hell."

Removing the goddamn tape was worse than the freaking tattoo. Silence was followed by the somber sounds of tears and sniffling.

"It's amazing," Mom said as she held up the actual photo next to him. "That's really him." Reincarnated by ink and talent, Michael clearly was there in the flesh. She then began to cry in an accelerated fashion, "Are you giving up on them bringing him home alive by getting this tattoo? What if he comes home alive, what will you do then?"

To ease her pain, I told her, "You know what, Ma, if he comes home alive, he would get a kick out of it and probably laugh at me for doing it prematurely, but I would still be honored to wear him on my back for having the bravery to survive."

I knew in my heart he was gone but had to keep her motivated by hope. This was making her get through the toughest days, for that second I was mad at myself for possibly being responsible for her questioning hope.

This was the first way I would honor his request. Thank you, Dave, for bringing a piece of Michael home to my family.

Four more agonizing nights passed, and it was now October 5, 2001. For the first twenty-two years of Michael's life, this was the day we celebrated his birthday. But his twenty-third birthday, just weeks after the attacks, would be the day the entire community celebrated his life though a memorial service. It would take place up the street from the home where we grew up, at Our Lady Star of the Sea church. He was still missing in action at the World Trade Center site, something incomprehensible to me.

As I donned my tapered, jet-black pinstripe suit, my eyes began to fill with tears as I envisioned what I would say as I gave the eulogy in his honor. My stomach turned at the thought of him being gone. *I have to get hold of myself; I owe it to Mike to keep my composure and honor him in a monumental way through a descriptive eulogy of what he meant to me, my family, and the entire community.* I closed my eyes, took a deep breath, and gazed deep into the mirror. It was at this very moment that I was overcome by severe survivor's guilt. *Why am I here, why is he gone?* Just a few short weeks ago he had been here telling me how much I was going to enjoy the fire department once I got on, how he was having the time of his life. Now he was missing, yet to be recovered, and the only item that would mark his existence on this earth would be a 24 in x 24 in photo of him in his firefighter bunker gear, positioned in the church on a gold easel that I was responsible for transporting and setting up at the foot of the altar.

A black stretch limousine pulled up to our house about 5:45 PM. I slowly followed the echoing cries of my family into the limousine. The half-mile ride to the church felt like a never-ending emotional journey. I prayed this was all just a bad nightmare.

As we exited the limousine as a family, I could not believe what I was seeing. Thousands of people had shown up to honor and say their last goodbyes to Michael. Hundreds of familiar and unfamiliar faces lined up and formed a makeshift canyon that would lead us to Michael's final mass.

Our family summoned Michael's closest friends to speak about him in the form of a eulogy. Jennifer, his girlfriend of seven years; John Didonato; Christopher Vallone; and Steven Sciarrino, all life-long friends of Michael had the duty of telling the story of one of the bravest young men to serve our nation on the morning of September 11, 2001.

The immediate family was seated in the front pew of the church on the left side of the aisle, facing the altar, while special dignitaries sat in the first pews to the right side of the aisle. Rudolph Giuliani, New York City's mayor at the time, was seated closest to the aisle and to the left of the city's fire commissioner, Thomas Von Essen. Other dignitaries from the community, as well as prominent public figures, filled the first, second, and third pews.

Monsignor Jeff Conway started the service. There was not an empty seat or dry eye in God's house that evening. He spoke about how heroes touch the lives of many, and how they make tremendous sacrifices during their own lives for the benefit of the ones closest to them, as well as for complete strangers. Although his words about life and heroism were comforting and shed temporary light on the situation, the truth of the matter was that it wasn't going to bring him back.

As the monsignor continued to speak of Michael, God, and sacrifice, I glanced over at the mayor and couldn't help but notice that he was looking at Michael's photo at the base of the altar, then looking at my parents, then back to the photo, and then to my family several times, and he shook his head in disbelief, probably about Michael's youth and the pain we were all going through at that moment of our lives. To see someone of Mayor Giuliani's stature express sincerity and care toward us during that moment was monumental.

Our family, seated in the front pew, was sobbing the entire time leading up to the eulogies. John Didonato was the first speaker. John was Michael's best friend. I vividly recall John walking up to the altar toward the podium; he resembled a person who was lost, not knowing where he was or what he was doing at the moment. As he began to speak, the opening words were clear, concise, and firm, but they quickly turned into the spoken emotions everyone was feeling deep inside. Overwhelmed by grief, he was barely able to complete a sentence. John spoke about all the great memories he had shared with my brother, and he made it clear to the people in attendance that he had never had a friend like Mike and that Mike would never be forgotten. It was clear to everyone that the pile of pages he brought forth to the podium were never read in their entirety. He was crippled by the loss of his best friend.

Chris Vallone, someone who shared a special relationship with not only Michael but me as well, headed to the podium next. Chris shared the same birthday as Michael, October 5. I can't imagine how hard it was for Chris to speak about the death of one of his closest friends on his own birthday. Tears of sadness spilled from his eyes and ran down his cheeks as he spoke about the earliest fishing trips we took as twelve-year-olds.

One of the most outstanding stories Chris spoke about was one experience Mike, Chris, and I shared, one that took place on a rainy summer morning at Arbutus Lake on July 23. We were either fourteen or fifteen years old. The forecast called for rain, but Chris and I disregarded the severity of the weatherman's predictions. Mike, prepared as always, was the only one who was smart enough to wear a raincoat. It started off as a cool mist. Suddenly, the skies darkened and the rain started to come down heavier. Within minutes it seemed like we were in the middle of a monsoon. Chris and I pleaded with him to share his grossly oversized yellow rubber raincoat with us so we could create a tent that could have easily sheltered us from the severe elements we were exposed to. He quickly rejected with a grin, stating, "No way, this tournament is mine. Get your money ready, boys; this one is going down in the books for me, baby."

Disgruntled for many reasons that day, Chris and I had succumbed to the devastation of the loss. Similarly, Chris's spirit succumbed to devastation as he continued to move through his speech. Reflecting back on Mike took a toll on him; he was breaking down as the eulogy went on. Chris concluded by saying, "On this day, our birthdays, Mike, I will forever light an extra candle for you in memory of the great life you lived."

A slender man of substantial height with salt-and-pepper hair, wearing the full dress uniform of the fire department, headed to the altar slowly as he wiped tears from his eyes. His name was Robert Annunziato. He was one of the senior men in Ladder Company

11. He began his eulogy in a humorous fashion. He reflected back on the first time Michael had come to the firehouse to introduce himself. He said, "As I was standing in front of the firehouse, a silver 2000 Infiniti Q45 with blacked-out windows pulled up to the apron of the firehouse driveway in a hurried manner. I didn't know if there was an emergency or I was going to be a victim of a drive-by shooting!" The people attending Mass burst into laughter. He went on to tell us how from that point on, Michael had always come to the firehouse prepared for duty. He was groomed, and his uniform was pressed as if he were in the military. He spoke about the strong bond he formed with Mike over the seven short weeks Michael was in the firehouse on his fire academy field training program. As Bobby wept, he went on to say, "I showed him the ropes, worked with him on drills, and cleaned tools with him until the wee hours of the night. I knew he was special; he wanted to learn the job and had a great passion for life. He was an all-star probie, and he should have never been taken from us so soon." As he concluded his eulogy, he looked toward the sky and said, "Mike, it was an honor to have worked alongside such a young hero; you will be forever missed."

As Bobby slowly took his seat, Mayor Giuliani headed toward the podium. Choked up with emotion, he started to speak about the brave men and woman who had bonded together that horrific day and how they had brilliantly executed the largest rescue effort in the history of our nation. He told the people he was proud of Michael, and he was impressed that a young man at the age of only twenty-two had charged forward with intentions of serving his city no matter if it meant him laying down his life. I couldn't believe this was happening; the mayor of the greatest city in the universe was honoring Mike in such an emotional way. He concluded by saying, "Michael will forever be an inspiration to me and this great nation of ours."

As the emotional rollercoaster of eulogies continued, Jennifer, Mike's girlfriend of seven years clutched the sides of the podium and took a deep breath to regain her composure. There was an apparent anxiety among the congregation; it seemed like all of them had the same thought in their minds: *How is she going to be able to get through this?*

In a quiet, softly spoken voice, she said, "There he was, with his red hair and chubby cheeks; he was adorable. We met when he was fifteen years old and I was fourteen. With no drivers licenses, and just a bus pass, Mike usually chose to rollerblade six miles to my house to come see me. That in itself proved to me that he truly loved me." She remained strong throughout the eulogy; it made me very proud to see she had that much strength within herself during that trying time. She clearly expressed the undying love and devotion that existed between them. The congregation seemed to be brought to their knees as she continued to elaborate on the lost love she will forever be without. "I love you always, Mike," she said as she descended the altar steps.

With the morbid atmosphere gaining momentum, Steven Sciarrino headed toward the microphone armed with a weathered scroll of memories in hand. He looked out upon the crowded pews in all directions, took a deep breath, and began. "As I stand here on the altar, about to speak about Michael, I look at the thousands of people that are here in attendance, and say to myself, 'What would Mike have thought about all of this?' What would he would have said about the attendance here in Our Lady Star of the Sea Church? And it would have been something like this: 'That's it? That's all the people who showed up?'"

This is the point in the ceremony where the tide turned. The crowd burst into laughter. He then continued. "As Michael would say, 'Hey, I'm not conceited; I am convinced.'" Chuckling, Steve went on by saying, "Mike definitely cared about his appearance. I remember going clothes shopping with him a lot, and him saying, 'I just want to stop in the sneaker store a second.' And I would be like, 'The sneaker store?' He already had about forty-seven pairs of mint-condition sneakers perfectly positioned on racks, but he didn't care; the light blue sneakers matched his jersey, so he was getting them.

"'One more for the collection,' he said."

The crowd's spirits were once again lifted up through the words of Steve. The tears of sadness now transitioned to the tears of laughter. "Mike had a way with the women! It was his way or no way, but they all loved him. But his heart was with his girlfriend, Jennifer, to the end.

"He was such a great athlete, but an unbelievable hockey player. I remember waiting for Turtle Pond to freeze every winter; we would play hockey from sunrise to sunset. Mike would skate around us like we weren't even there. Goal after goal, he was the man. Very competitive, mainly with his brother Joe, but also with everything he did, he gave it a hundred percent. I remember playing the video game NHL 91 for the Sega Genesis game console and me getting so mad; he was the only one who could beat me, but he probably pulled my controller out when I wasn't looking. He was a silent ball breaker.

"Hours we would spend listening to music, driving around in our cars. Those were some of the best times I had, talking about life and joking around. I remember specifically one incident that stands out in my mind, when he came into my place of work, excited to share the news that he was a New York City firefighter, and me striking a book of matches, saying, 'May this be the biggest blaze you ever put out.' He then stomped it out with a smile. Unfortunately it wasn't his last. And even though we are all hurting inside, we have to all remember, Michael didn't have to be a firefighter, he wanted to be one, and on September 11, he died a hero. In life, people pass, but memories never die, and for that I am grateful, because Mike left me with some of the greatest memories I will ever have. I'll miss you always; I love you, Mike."

As Steve took his seat next to my father, I walked up to the altar with a head full of memories. I grabbed the microphone, cleared my throat, and gazed out to the pews in complete amazement of the fact that my kid brother had touched all these lives. "Michael was my best friend ..."

A few sleepless nights later, about 2:30 AM, after waking from my usual anxiety episode, I went to the kitchen to pour myself a glass of cold water with hopes of cooling my sweaty body when it hit me. Crusty-eyed and drenched with sweat, I ran into my bedroom, in the pitch-black, to wake Maria. "Maria, Maria, wake up!"

Startled and scared, she looked at me with nervousness and asked, "What happened, what's wrong?"

I told her I had an idea. "I know what else we can do that will forever make his spirit live on. I want to get the street named after him, I want to get them to recognize him on the block he grew up on, Kingdom Avenue."

The morning after, I woke with the daily exhaustion that had become part of my life over the last month and a half, and while at breakfast, I strategically and verbally mapped out a plan of what the first steps should be to bring this idea to reality. I knew I would have to start right there on the very street we grew up on, hitting the pavement with Maria and Jenna going door to door, petition in hand, explaining to the neighborhood what my intentions were, who Michael was if they didn't know him, what he did, and why. As a community, we owed it to him to recognize the sacrifices he made for the world.

It was Sunday, and I began my quest the moment I left the front door of my house. After five long hours, we had gone door to door and spoke with all the homeowners. We had a success rate of 98 percent. Four pages of legal-size paper stated the exact addresses and names of the residents, followed by their signatures. It was a great success; they all agreed that we should have the street recognized after him.

From this point forward, I knew we would have to work with local politicians and government officials to get this passed. At that time Maria had been employed by the Staten Island Economical Development Corporation, under the leadership of Caesar J.Claro, who assisted by providing us with the names of local politicians we needed to help us get through the channels.

But first we had to get the South Community Board 3 to hear my case and vote on it with their support for us to move on.

On a cool autumn night in October, I arrived at the community board meeting with hopes of having the microphone in order to state my case. Within minutes, John Antonello and Matthew Sciarrino ESQ, both public figures in the community, walked me up to the microphone and introduced me as the brother of Staten Island's youngest firefighter who was missing at the World Trade Center site.

Immediate silence struck the room. I grabbed the microphone with crushing force; I didn't want my sweaty hands to let it slip away. This was my one and only chance to get this done. "My name is Joseph Cammarata. I am the brother of one of the most honorable men that has walked this earth. Someone, at the tender age of twenty-two years old, made the supreme sacrifice just a few short weeks ago. In a letter he left in his nightstand before the attacks, he left four last requests in his letter titled, 'If anything ever happens to me.' In it, he wrote,

"'1. Take care of Jenna'

"'2. Don't mourn me as this is the career I chose'

"'3. Make my spirit live on'

"'4. Remember I love you all and will be waiting for you upstairs.'"

I looked into the crowd and saw women and men brought to tears. "Ladies and gentleman of the board, it is number 3, 'Make my spirit live on,' that brings me before you here tonight. I take his request as an obligation, something I will relentlessly pursue my entire life. I have in my hand a petition with 98 percent of the residents of the street we grew up on who support me in my efforts. Tonight, I ask you for support, the community which shaped the character of this special person, my brother, my hero, by honoring his last request of making his spirit live on. Thank you and God bless."

I grabbed the signed petition, and before I could take one step, the entire room stood in applause for what seemed to be an eternity. On completion, I was told they would vote on it right then and there.

All I heard was yea, yea, yea, yea, and yea. It was unanimously passed, just like that, right in front of me. The feeling was unbelievable.

This was just the beginning of the hard work that lay ahead. Working closely with Maria, we sought help from South Shore City Council member Andrew Lanza. On the news of the community board's passage of it unanimously, he sat with us and started the process to draft it for legislation for the request, with the hope to have it before the Parks and Recreation Committee for a vote by the following week. When he was asked about our quest by the press, he stated, "I don't see an impediment to this happening. I think it will be a nice tribute to the family. Michael Cammarata did a lot for his community." I was grateful to hear we had his support.

Once we passed unanimously with Parks and Recreation, we had to take it through the channels of the Department of Transportation and then the mayor's office.

The battle had just begun, and the anxiety surrounding me about achieving the success of this quest was enormous. Besides the usual rituals I faced trying to sleep, I now found myself paralyzed with anxiety over this as well.

Day by day, we checked the progress with Lanza's office. No news yet. The anticipation was running high until one day, Maria came home with the news: we got passed by the D.O.T. The mayor's office was the only thing standing in our way of making his spirit live on in a big way.

A wise man once told me, "You prepared the cake, put it in the oven, and now you have to be patient while the cake bakes." He was referring to my being patient while I awaited the response from the mayor's office.

While our group of pioneers was standing by for an answer, Andrew Lanza was asked by the press, "What if every family of a 9-11 victim wants a street sign, what will you do then?" He answered, "I don't see the downside of doing this. If it's three thousand signs we need, then it's three thousand signs! We constantly have this as a reminder. We need to set these people apart, put them on a pedestal as heroes so that children and future generations will not forget them."

If this came to fruition, I would be responsible for hundreds of families sharing a piece of Michael as a result of his letter. The feeling was amazing.

A few short days later, I was notified our hard work and efforts had paid off. We got it! We did it! The feeling was immeasurable. People believed in my idea; they believed in Michael and what he stood for. His sign would be the first one of hundreds hung in the city. His letter inspired me to make his spirit live on, and as a result of his courage to put pen to paper and write that letter, others will have their family members immortalized within the city forever.

Official street renaming
My family, local firefighters, and politicians Vito Fossella and Andrew Lanza

Chapter 6

Six Empty Chairs

Seven weeks since Michael was officially declared missing, we were notified by the fire department that the graduation for Michael's probie class was going to be on November 2, 2001, at Brooklyn College. He wasn't going to be able to attend; he was still buried in the rubble and hadn't been found. We had to go on his behalf; this was what he would want us to do. But how was my family going to hold up?

My family got in the car; we drove in complete silence to Jen's house to pick her up. This was going to be a rough day. I knew once we got to the ceremony and my mother saw the other probies with their families, smiling and taking pictures, she was going to break down. We all were. This wasn't supposed to be like this.

These types of ceremonies are supposed to be filled with joy and happiness. For us, the feeling was bittersweet.

The day was absolutely gorgeous; the foliage on the grounds of the campus was breathtaking. We held hands as a family and walked to the auditorium, observing our surroundings, making small talk about the atmosphere that was acting as a buffer, covering our emotions from exposing themselves before we entered the building. As much as I wanted to break down at every one of these events that were honoring Mike, I couldn't. I had to be the centurion to my family, even if I was crumbling from the inside out. Bottling up my emotions on a daily basis eventually would catch up with me, but right now, the façade I was projecting served a greater purpose.

On check in, we were ushered to the second row of the auditorium. I noticed immediately that we were sitting behind what seemed to be seating for dignitaries or VIPs. There were six seats cordoned off by roping that you would see in a theater. Also, I noticed that they had some sort of drapery on the seats, resembling something that royalty would be seated on. My curiosity got the better of me at this point. I walked up to the front row to see who I was sitting behind. Maybe it was Thomas Von Essen, the fire commissioner; Rudy Giuliani, the mayor of New York City; or someone else of high status.

I noticed white name tags on the seats, and as my eyes came into focus, the names started to become legible. The names read Charlie Anaya, Richard Allen, Anthony Rodriguez, Andrew

Brunn, Michael Cammarata, and Michael D'Auria. The six chairs were draped with black and purple bunting, a traditional sign of mourning within the fire department, recognizing those who have fallen. I immediately became weak in the knees, and tears filled my eyes. I no longer could read these names, and they became more and more blurry as each tear filled my eyes. These chairs were empty. This couldn't be real; they are the first probies never to make graduation. This wasn't fair.

The auditorium filled to capacity, as did my mind with visions of Mike still crushed by millions of tons of debris. Sitting in that auditorium before the ceremony, staring at those empty chairs temporarily stifled any enthusiasm or drive I had to become a firefighter. These young men died on this job as probies. They never had the chance to experience the best things this job had to offer. I'd better be sure I still wanted to do this. The pressure from my family to stray from my dream was as enormous as the overwhelming emotions I had staring at those empty chairs.

The ceremony started with complete and utter silence from the audience. Everyone heard the same thing: the bells. Four sets of five bells that signified a firefighter has died in the line of duty, a sound that continuously replays in my mind day after day. We all started to get choked up. I found myself fighting my emotions from displaying themselves. And then the bagpipes followed. I lost it. My mother once again buried her head in my father chest, a familiar sight to me, one that ripped out my heart. I glanced over at my father, and he was crying. My father was a man I have always looked at as being tough as nails. He was always a hero to me, and that day, as on 9-11, my hero was brought to his knees, something no one should ever see.

The six families, each of us representing the souls who were supposed to be occupying those chairs, were all present to accept a diploma posthumously for our loved ones. We were individually called to the stage to accept their certificates.

There he was—Rudy, America's mayor—supporting us once again, this time to present us, the family of Michael Cammarata, with a diploma on his behalf. The audience, most in tears, stood in ovation for more than a minute, followed by a moment of silence and then more applauding. I shook Mr. Giuliani's hand; he looked me in the eyes with a tremendous sense of sincerity and said, "You truly are courageous for following in Michael's footsteps to become a firefighter. If you ever need anything, don't hesitate to contact me." I thanked him for his support and, at that point, was so inspired to continue with my dream, I couldn't envision anything impeding it.

Mr. Giuliani went on to speak to the graduating class. "You've been a source of tremendous inspiration. The people who died on September 11 died as military heroes. They were defending America. We always knew we had the best fire department in the world. Now, nobody doubts that." Those words served as a source of comfort for my entire family.

In the days that followed, I found myself grappling with many questions. Was I still doing this because I always wanted to since childhood? Should I reassess my thought of becoming a fire-fighter? After all, the game had changed since the eleventh and Mike's death. Did my desire to join the department intensify after Michael's untimely death on the eleventh? Those questions would consume the several sleepless nights I encountered.

Night after night, the six chairs, covered with bunting, became still frames in my dreams. The thought of possibly dying and my mother and father having to come to my graduation, staring at another empty chair their son was supposed to fill, terrified me. How would they go on if something happened to me?

I will never be able to look at an empty chair the same way again.

Chapter 7

Filling His Boots

It was New Year's Eve 2001. I was supposed to reflect on the good and bad of the previous year. I was at my parents' home with my fiancée, sister Kim, Nanny Josephine, and parents, watching the Dick Clark show. I couldn't wait for this ball to drop and for 2001 to be over.

You could even see a look of pessimism on Dick Clark's face; he had the hardest job in the world that night. He was going to be the one ushering in the New Year, telling everyone in the city, "Happy New Year," at midnight. But what the fuck was there to be happy about? The ball was about to drop in Times Square in New York City, where more than two thousand people had lost their lives fifteen short weeks ago. But the festivities had to go on; we had to show the world, especially those who were responsible for the tragedy, that we were stronger as a nation. However, it was still hard for anyone in New York City to stay optimistic, especially me, when my brother was buried in the rubble, under millions of tons of debris.

Dick Clark started his countdown—ten, nine, eight, seven, six—and the tears of grief started to flow from my eyes. I looked around the living room and saw my mother's head buried in my father's chest. She was crying, pleading for God to bring Michael home to her in the upcoming New Year. She wanted her baby recovered; I wanted my brother back. Five, four, three; I should be ecstatic, celebrating with Michael right now. Yesterday I had gotten word I would be sworn in as the bravest in two weeks. Two, one; but he wasn't here to celebrate with me and bust my chops. I wasn't even happy that night. Happy New Year! I poured the champagne, requested my family to raise their glasses, and I toasted to Michael. "To Michael, our hero forever, someone who will be watching over us for the years to come, someone who will be waiting for us upstairs. It was a privilege for us to call you family. We love you." The feeling then transitioned to feeling that the one good thing, the goal I had been striving for my whole life, was days away, and I wasn't focused. I was not even happy.

It was January 14, 2002, the day I had been waiting for my entire life. I was headed to Randall's Island, the firefighting training academy, also known as the "Rock," to be sworn in. This was the very facility where my brother took his oath and trained just a few months before the morning of September 11.

I found myself envisioning what Michael must have been feeling that morning he was sworn in. Nervousness, anxiety, happiness, and excitement probably filled his soul, as he walked through the facility gates. These were the absolute opposite feelings that I had.

Besides the bitter sweetness that would be expected, I knew I had a mission to complete. I had to fill the boots of my brother. I had to walk the very same steps that he did, with one thing in mind: to become the Bravest. But a few things haunted me in the back of my mind. Not only did Michael die on the job just eighteen weeks ago, he was still buried in the rubble. This was an enormous weight I had to carry while staying focused on the training that lay ahead in the upcoming months. Was I going to be able to get a handle on this negativity in my life and complete this mission?

I was not the only one in my probie class in this situation. Timothy Riches and Joe Pansini were also in the exact position I was in. They also lost their brothers, who were firefighters. Brian Stack, also a probie in the same boat as us, lost his father, who was a battalion chief. The four of us were invited on the stage in the auditorium to take the oath on behalf of our entering probie class. We then raised our right hands and were sworn in by the newly elected mayor, Michael Bloomberg, and newly appointed fire commissioner, Nicholas Scoppetta.

Mayor Bloomberg didn't downplay the high risk of fighting fires. He went on to tell us, "You've accepted a fundamentally dangerous job." At that point, that very second, I had an intense flashback of the towers collapsing. Sitting in my seat, I actually recalled smelling the burning and decomposed flesh that I smelled the morning of September 11, 2001. I almost had to get up and wash my face with cold water, but I didn't want anyone to notice the distressed look upon my face. So I sat still until the sweat on my face dried and the heavy breathing stopped.

After the dignitaries were ushered out and the ceremony concluded, so did the happy occasion. We were welcomed by the staff at the academy in an unorthodox fashion. First, the captain of Probie School came in, telling us to enjoy the next twelve days until the first day of training on the twenty-seventh. "Be prepared to come in here and work like dogs. You are walking among the spirits of the men who gave their lives for the people of this city. Anyone who thinks they are going to try and coast through Probie School and not work hard is disrespecting the great men who trained here before you and laid down their lives selflessly for others." While the captain was speaking, a man dressed in firefighter attire walked around, pulling probies out of their seats, making them do pushups, screaming at them, referring to them as disrespectful probies, "Get down and give me fifty." These probies were blasting out pushups in their dress suits; this resembled a scene out of the movie *Full Metal Jacket.*

The captain continued, "If you complain now, or from this point forward, you should take a look of these four men who stood up here today and took the oath before you, the ones who lost family on 9-11. Take a good look at them; I bet they won't be complaining. I am an expert at weeding out the assholes. Don't be an asshole like these screw-ups who are being made examples of by doing pushups. If you slack off, I will find you and make your life a living fucking hell." He walked off the stage, toward the back of the auditorium, and slammed the door with crushing force.

The next member of the training facility introduced himself. He was the madman who was ranting and forcing probies to do pushups, screaming at the top of his lungs, "I am Drill Instructor Moriarity." A former Marine, groomed as precisely as a mannequin, serious as a heart attack in his stature, said, "I am not here to make friends. I am here to police your every move. Don't be like these fellow probies of yours, doing pushups in suits. They are fuck-ups; they won't last here very long, ladies and gentlemen. I am here to make your visit here at Probie School as uncomfortable as humanly possible. I have one thing to say: if you make it through this treacherous training program without me knowing your name, probies, you done good. I will be waiting for you here on the twenty-seventh. The gates open at 0500 hours. Be mustered up with fully shaved heads. That includes you, Probie Smith [the only female probie in the class], in company order by 0630 hours for a head-to-toe full inspection. Don't be late, probies." He stormed out of the room, as had the captain. We were left in the auditorium scared, silent, and with no further direction. It was a good ten minutes before any of us had the balls to get out of our seats and leave.

When I walked out of the auditorium, the drill instructor called my name. "Probie Cammarata, Probie Cammarata." I hurried over to him, scared shitless he was going to rip into me. He told me,

"The captain wants to see you in his office." At that moment, I felt like I would shit my pants. What the fuck did I do that the captain wanted to see me? I was yes sirring and no sirring everyone that day. I was sure I was walking a straight line.

When I walked into the office, the captain was sitting behind his desk. He said, "Your brother, I remember him; he was a standout probie, a good kid." He went on. "Listen, I got about ten news reporters outside. They want to interview you. If you want, you can speak to them. You don't have to answer their questions if you don't want to. I'll tell them to beat it. It's up to you."

I took their questions. They wanted to know about Michael and what it was like to be following in the his footsteps and those of all the heroes who gave their lives that day. I felt obligated to keep his spirit and name alive by honoring him with the press on hand.

The week and a half before the first training day I spent preparing myself mentally for the clear challenges that lay ahead. The sleepless nights and flashbacks started to intensify. They were beginning to control my emotions to a point where I found myself scared of the future. Was this a sign of the fate ahead of me? Was this Michael's way of trying to make me reconsider? Night after night, I woke several times during the night, stricken by silence and a racing heart, the same way I was when I sifted through that wreckage that September day. I found myself constantly wondering if this was about my childhood dreams or proving to the world I had the courage to charge forward even though Michael was lost. I couldn't talk to anyone about this; I didn't want anyone to question my courage. I kept my emotions bottled up, and the pressure was building every single minute that went by. Was I going to follow through with this? Did I have what it took to fill Michael's boots and continue our family legacy with the NYC Fire Department?

Chapter 8

In the Shadow of Giants

It was 0434 hours on the morning of January 27, 2002. I was freezing,
standing out in front of my home, anxiously awaiting my carpool
to arrive to take me to my first day of training at the Rock. Known
as Randall's Island to the general population of the city, we probies
referred to it as the Rock because of its resemblance to Alcatraz. The
geography mirrored Alcatraz in many aspects. Randall's Island was
positioned off the shore of Manhattan, surrounded by treacherous
crosscurrents and choppy water. We all knew there was no escaping
the facility once we entered. We knew we had to get through the
day ahead of us. I looked at it as if I was imprisoned from 0630
hours to 1700 hours daily. But when released, the reward of being
a rehabilitated soul, a determined, fine-tuned firefighter was worth
the four-month training sentence that lay ahead. I considered this

light time, as there was a light at the end of the tunnel. After all, this should be easy; I have been incarcerated by my emotions since 9-11, with a psychological sentence of life.

Tommy Hunt and John Baggs, two fellow probies, arrived at my house about a quarter to five. We spoke briefly about the excitement of our first day and then were quickly swallowed up by the alleged rumors of what the first day was going to be like. I told them I remembered a few months ago, when Michael came home from his first day of training, he told me how hard it was. They pushed him almost to his breaking point on an 85 degree day. He also told me that twenty guys were throwing up violently before the day was over, and there were no breaks. On top of that, they had fifteen minutes to eat lunch, three hours of physical training, followed by three hours of classroom and three hours of firefighting techniques. As we got closer, we flirted with the idea of turning around and going home, but none of us wanted to back down to the challenges of the Rock.

We parked the car and got out, and I remember being greeted by the frigid wind chill, a feeling that is only recognized by those who have done a stint on the Rock. We heard screaming a few hundred yards away. As we got closer, the voice was that of Moriarity, that aggressive drill instructor from the swearing in, relentlessly riding a probie for crossing the threshold of the facility, probably for not showing the proper respect necessary. We all stopped and conducted our own visual inspections of our uniforms. Tommy noticed my badge was slightly crooked on my hat, and I told Baggs to straighten his gig line. Tommy looked like he could do a modeling shoot for recruitment, his uniform was so tight.

We cautiously approached what we believed was the entrance. There were no lights; it was so dark the only guidance we had was that madman's voice. We passed what appeared to be fifteen-foot rusted gates. We guessed this was the entrance.

Hunt mumbled, "Guys, this place looks much different in the dark." We now were property of the Rock.

We walked a few more feet to be greeted by a drill instructor counting at the top of his lungs, "Forty-one, forty-one, forty-one. You don't get it, probie, your chest must hit the floor. Forty-one, forty-one, forty-two. Look, you follow directions."

We sneakily walked past him into the tubular entrances into the facility. I looked at my watch; it was 0545 hours, and the damn sun wasn't even up yet. We were forty-five minutes early, and that probie was being disciplined. We quickly learned a lesson on the first day: stay in the car until ten minutes before muster so we can avoid that madman drill instructor until the day officially starts.

It was time for our daily roll call at 0645 hours. The drill instructor stood on a ten-foot platform. This enabled him to have a bird's-eye view of all his probies, mustering within the ranks. This gave him the ability to see each and every breath we took. He then asked every squad leader for their head counts. If all were present, they had to respond, "All present and accounted for, sir." A few probies ran past the gates and into the ranks. The drill instructor ordered them to the platform. He quickly started a mini calisthenics group for the late guys. I remember thinking, *This is going to be a long day, and a long four months.*

After roll call, my squad filed down the metal tubular entranceway into the facility. I stopped and stared at this sign crookedly hung on the wall. It gave me chills like I had never had in my entire life. It read, "Let no man's ghost come back and say that my training let me down." This phrase became etched in my mind until this very day. Mike's training didn't let him down. You couldn't have trained for that incident; it wasn't supposed to have happened like that. Why did they send in all those men?

Surprisingly, the day moved along quite fast. I had moved through the classroom and firefighting tactics sessions, had lunch, and had changed into my PT gear for my speed and agility session. After a weigh in, we were going to be timed on our mile and a half run, pushups, sit-ups, and pull-ups.

"Cammarata, weight 230, body fat 26 percent." Lieutenant Casiola screamed out my measurements, followed by, "Your brother was about 175 and 7 percent. What's the deal, probie?"

"I am forty pounds over my normal weight. I packed on forty after the eleventh."

"No excuse, probie. You out of all people should have come here prepared. Pushups, probie, one minute, go."

I did twenty-six, barely making the requirement of twenty-five.

"Okay, probie, sit-ups, one minute, go."

I just made thirty-five, the requirement.

Next was pull-ups. I couldn't even do one. I was shocked. He asked me what I did the run in. I told him 11:59, one second before the cutoff.

He told me, "Your brother did this exact run in 10:23. You're not even close!"

I made the requirements by the skin of my teeth. He then called attention to the class and told everyone, "Cammarata came to this academy prepared just enough to get by these events. He should have been more prepared than all of you. His brother was an extraordinary probie who I had the pleasure of training just a few months ago. He was the youngest man we lost in the Trade Center. His brother Michael came here in great shape; Joseph did not."

This man didn't embarrass me; he motivated me to strive for excellence, to push myself physically and mentally to the limits. I had a passionate feeling in my soul; I would turn my act around and prove to Casiola that I was able to fill Michael's boots! I was confident I could return to the weight I was when I took the physical, 190 pounds of brute force. It would be tough. I would have to battle my emotions first and then the weight to be successful.

After battling fires the first day, I then had to battle traffic. I arrived home about 1700 hours, exhausted and bombarded with homework. I had to shower, eat, and try to keep my eyes open enough to complete my work and studies. I was in bed by 2000 hrs. I had to wake up and do it all over again the next day.

As time went on, I started to get into a routine to cope with the strenuous days I was going through. I started a study group with some of the greatest guys in my squad. Our group consisted of Phil Pape, a fitness guru; Tommy Hunt, a Justin Timberlake look-alike; Mike Childs, who reminded me of the Riddler from *Batman*; Lou Giovanazzo, the crazy, redheaded Italian who always had the answers; and last but not least, the glue behind the gang, Davey Boy Vormitag. I was called the Professor, named by Louie G for creating test questions that always showed up on the test. We forged a bond that was able to deflect any negativity the stresses of the academy produced. These became my best friends; they eased the pain of envisioning what Michael's every move had been as I went through the same process that Mike had just a few months earlier.

As time started to pass, we were becoming fine-tuned young men and women. My pace started to pick up on the run because of Hunt, and my pushups, sit-ups, and pull-ups were improving as a result of the push from Pape. He monitored my fitness and nutrition throughout the day. If he saw me eating something unhealthy, he said, "Remember the run. If you want to crush it, you can't be a disgusting fat body." I returned the favor by holding daily study groups during lunch, predicting questions as if I was Nostradamus, except my success rate was much higher than his. I also returned the favor to Hunt for training me on our off days for the run by tutoring him at my home, and within weeks, his scores rose to the top of the class.

It became evident, although we were only probies at the Rock, that we were forming our own brotherhood that would last a lifetime. We relied on each other to get through the rough and choppy days that resembled the currents that surround the Rock.

As time went on, the tests got harder and the runs got longer. I think we were actually approaching ten miles a day, and the firefighting tactics became more demanding; we were pushing ourselves to the limits. For four months straight, none one of us saw our friends or families. We ate, slept, and lived with our new brothers.

We were quickly approaching hell week. All of our written and physical exams would take place over five consecutive days. There also was the hurdle of the state test. You can make it all the way through Probie School, pass everything, and if you fail the state test, you don't become a firefighter. Not one member on the job ever failed the state exam. I didn't want to be the first, and neither did anyone else.

The pressure was building; I hadn't seen my fiancée in weeks. I was so committed to carrying out my dream that I didn't let anyone or anything interfere. I was committed, driven beyond belief to rip through hell week. I had to take the exams by the horns—especially the physical aspect of the testing I originally had problems with—and control my destiny. I had to capture my dream once and for all. I had inspiration on my side: the greatest person who ever roamed the earth, my brother, my hero, Michael.

I wasn't even nervous. I didn't sleep one wink all week. I was running on pure adrenaline. I knocked out all the written firefighter exams and state certifications. It was the last day, and the only thing standing in my way were the original hurdles: the run, pushups, sit-ups, and pull-ups. I weighed in at 207 pounds and with 13 percent body fat, a tremendous drop. First were the pushups. I did forty-eight in a minute, shattering the requirement of twenty-five. Next I had to tackle the sit-ups. I previously did thirty-five; this time, forty-nine. Now for the pull-ups. Casiola reminded me I couldn't do one the last time and that if I didn't do five this time, I wouldn't make it.

I said, "I need five minutes. I'll be right back." I ran to put on my full bunker gear and boots, not required for testing, but I wanted to prove a point. I came back to the rusted, bent pull-up bar in my bunker gear and helmet.

He looked at me and asked, "In bunker gear?" I was ready! "Begin, Probie Cammarata."

My friends started to root me on. "One for the engine, two for the truck, three for squad, four for rescue, five for marine, six for the battalion." I started to weaken. "Seven for those who have fallen, eight for Michael, nine for Michael." I was now grunting. "Ten for Miccchhaaael, eleven for Casiola, twelve for brothers." I was screaming, grunting in pain. "Thirteen for the drill instructor."

I did it—thirteen—and screamed out everyone who inspired me to overcome a huge challenge. I only had the run, which I made by one second last time, standing in my way. Twelve minutes is the requirement; I had done it in 11:59. I had to do this.

The gun went off, and we ran as a group. Hunt started pacing me to do it in 11:30. I wanted him to push me harder, and he escalated to complete it in 11:00 flat by the second lap. I kept my legs going like a locomotion steaming full speed ahead. With every stride I envisioned throwing more coal into the fire that was fueling my soul, with the purpose of excelling. I started to push past my pacing partner. I was rounding the last bend, and as the vision of the finish line approached in the distance I passed Pape. I was sprinting so fast I could have sworn someone or something, maybe Michael, was propelling me forward. As I approached the finish line, my fellow probies who finished ahead of me were cheering me on. I charged to the finish, pushing myself beyond any limit that stood before me. I passed the finish line and kept running. I broke down in tears. I knew an angel had pushed me past that line. I knew Michael was rooting me on and played a part in my success over the past months. Everyone huddled around me, cheering for me as if I was a champion who had triumphed and overcome emotional and physical boundaries.

Casiola whispered in my ear, "Ten-fifteen. Michael would be proud of you. Good job, probie. See you at Brooklyn College for graduation."

I hugged him and told him he had been an inspiration that first day.

He said, "I did it for a reason: I knew you would achieve greatness." He added, "We will be passing your brother's badge down to you that day, so you can actively carry on your family's legacy in the fire department. No one will ever forget him."

This was one of the proudest days of my life. I felt an amazing power radiate throughout my entire body. I was forever going to have a piece of Michael protecting me while I was a firefighter, his badge, #1138.

It had been my uncle's badge since 1963, passed to my brother in 2001, and now was being given to me in 2002. I will always hold my head up high knowing great men have wore this badge. I will forever wear it with great honor.

None of us ever lost sight of the fact that six probies from the class before 9-11 gave their lives, one of them my brother Michael. We knew by going through our training that we were making their legacy live on. We were all proud to be following the footsteps of 343 great men who laid down their lives without thinking twice. Let's face it: we were getting closer to being great; we were doing it in the shadow of giants.

Chapter 9

First Impression

As I drove home from my graduation at Brooklyn College, fresh out of Probie School, still wet behind the ears, I found myself nervously planning my first visit to my new assignment. Engine Company 157 of Port Richmond, in Staten Island, New York, was where I wanted to go.

First impressions are everything at a new job, but in the fire department, a bad first impression will haunt you your entire twenty-year career. First and foremost, you'd better be "knocking on the door of the firehouse with your elbows." This is fire department lingo for bringing in food for the brothers. If you have a hand available for knocking, you probably didn't bring enough. Walking into the firehouse to meet the brothers as a new member, especially as a probie, should never be taken lightly. You have to prove yourself the minute you cross the threshold of the firehouse.

Carrying the weight of this and filling Michael's boots was tremendous. I couldn't be an average probie; I was walking in the shadow of a giant, someone who will be forever put on a pedestal in his brother's eyes and someone who made the supreme sacrifice. In plain English, I had the pressure of proving to everyone I could walk on water, and if I didn't know how, I'd better start learning. I had to report for duty in few short hours.

With the pressure mounting, I had a plan in place. It was 0900 hours the day before I had to be present for duty; I was in Brooklyn picking up lunch for the brothers. Armed with a six-foot hero, half Italian, and half American, plus all the trimmings, I headed to the firehouse to try to win over my future brothers by feeding them. After all, firemen love to eat. I made sure I was arriving unannounced. If I were to call in advance, they would be prepared for me, planning the practical jokes and initiation tactics that are common on the job.

Dressed in my fire department dress uniform, with shoes shined and uniform pressed, I knocked with my elbows. Footsteps echoed from inside the firehouse, as if someone was coming down a long hallway. It sounded like someone was dragging their boots, scraping them on a concrete floor; they got louder as the person neared the door.

"Who is it?" asked a raspy, smoke-eater's voice.

"Joe Cammarata. I am the new probie for the engine."

Still talking to me behind the red steel firehouse entry door, the man said, "Probie, are you joking? We haven't gotten a probie in almost twenty years."

Holding a six-foot sandwich, with shiny tins filled with salads and five bottles of soda at my feet, I was sweating, hoping this mysterious figure would open the door.

Finally, the door slowly creaked open. I simultaneously looked up just to make sure they weren't going to dump a huge bucket of water on me from the roof (a firehouse tradition and joke). A short figure, full of energy and knowledge like the doorman from the *Wizard of Oz* looked at me in disbelief, as I was standing there overwhelmed with the amount of food I was guarding.

He said, "Come right in, probie, and let me give you a hand." He helped me to the kitchen with the spread. Sitting around the table were four hungry, burly members of the firehouse. They told me the engine was out getting the meal; they would try to turn it around so we would eat the lunch I brought. Sure enough, the engine was on its way back.

I was now sitting in the kitchen, sweating profusely as they fired off questions to me. Finally, the whos, whats, wheres, whens, and whys were behind us—well until the engine got back and asked me the same questions.

As the members returned, I was greeted by my new company. A gray-haired man, full of sarcasm, told me I could have brought more food. I knew he had to be joking; I brought enough food to feed the whole country of Ethiopia. The ball breaking had started already. All eyes were on me. I was the new guy in town.

Sitting at that table, feeling extremely out of place, the men were actually being nice to me. I was being treated as one of the brothers. They asked me about Michael and if he had been recovered. I was shocked to see they knew so much about him, since he was only on the job a few weeks. They knew everything about me, too. I guess these guys did their homework on me before they would let me be assigned to their house.

Once we got past the awkwardness and finished the meal, I headed over to the sink to do the dishes. I rolled up my sleeves and turned on the water. The men all got up and told me they got it, sit down. I thought they might be testing me to see what I was made of. I continued to do the dishes until the senior man on duty, Bobby Caputo, told me, "Today you are our guest. You brought the meal. Sit down, and don't piss us off on the first day."

In the background, another guy said, "Don't get used to that, probie. After today you'll be eating, sleeping, and shitting in that sink." All the members on duty in that kitchen burst out in laughter, but I had experience with this type of atmosphere. After all, I pledged Alpha Upsilon Fraternity at St. John's University in the mid-1990s. I was tarred, feathered, and turned into a chicken cutlet at the beach. This should be a walk in the park.

It was showtime—roll call on the apparatus floor. It was my first day. I assumed the position as the backup to the nozzle man, the lead firefighter into the fire, the one responsible for controlling where the water goes to extinguish the fire. I was nervous. What if we got a fire tonight? Would I be prepared?

Immediately after roll call, a bleach white-haired experienced firefighter with terrible glasses, Neil Fitzpatrick, pulled me to the side and introduced himself. At the time, I did not know that the engine captain, Richie Scarpato, had strategically scheduled Neil to work by my side every tour. Neil was a pool of wisdom, which he was willing to splash his senior man knowledge onto me, things that our education at the academy could never afford us.

It became evident he was looking out for me. He showed me the ropes, where everything was in the firehouse; he introduced me to the men as well as their notorious pet peeves. Not only did I have to know the names of the men I was going to be living with, it would behoove me to know their pet peeves. I didn't want to piss anyone off.

The first night I never slept. I didn't want to go into the bunk-room to rest; I didn't want to risk missing a run. I awaited my first fire like a child waits for Santa Claus on Christmas Eve. Not that I ever wished the destruction of fire on anyone or their property, I just wanted to put my training to the test. I wanted to help people.

It was 0300 hours. I was sitting in the kitchen of the firehouse, wondering what Michael's first night had been like. I found out from the brothers in his firehouse, Engine 28 Ladder 11, that he never slept in the bunkroom. If he was to rest, he would lie on the couch in the kitchen. When the tone alarms would sound in the middle of the night and the company would be dispatched, they would slide down the brass pole from the second floor and come storming out the doors, which would wake him if necessary. I found myself following his strategy.

As time passed in the firehouse, I started to get into the swing of things. Even though I was being cleansed at least four to five times a tour by mysterious bucketfuls of water, I knew it was all good. If they didn't take the time to play practical jokes on me, that would mean they didn't like me.

Neil would pull me to the side every tour, drilling my knowledge of the tools and the rig. When finished, we would clean the fire engine. This would show great company pride, and after all, it was my job to do it every tour.

A probie should always be busy. If you had time to think or had spare time, you were doing something wrong. I anxiously awaited my first fire. I wanted to get past any fears of what the real deal would be like, as well as be christened into the department.

When the tone alarm rang, the rush I got as a probie was intense. When the call of a possible fire was announced over the loudspeaker in the firehouse, my heart would race, pounding with tremendous force. If you were standing next to me at the time this was happening, you wouldn't even need a stethoscope to hear my heartbeat. I would race to the pole, slide down, suit up piece by piece, and be on the rig within seconds, racing to the scene.

A few months passed. I was starting to prove myself and fit in at the firehouse. However, the pressure from Maria and my mother to reconsider my plans to be a firefighter was enormous. It had only been a few months, Michael was still missing, and now I was on the job. It was understandable that this pressure existed. Another pressure present within my soul was my desperate need to show my new brothers I had what it took to fight a real fire. There were fires that our company responded to, but when I was working, nothing had happened for the last three months.

It was a hot summer day, the day before my twenty-fifth birthday. I was present for duty at 0930 hours. Ninety-seven degrees and humid, this is the worst situation for firefighters to be in if a fire breaks out. I was cleaning tools when the tone alarms went off, and the computerized voice said, "Engine, Ladder," followed by the urgent voice of experience, twenty-year veteran Eddie Schyler. "Phone alarm, fire on the second floor of a private dwelling, 21 Palmer Ave., receiving multiple calls, sounds like a job, guys." I ran to my bunker gear to suit up, feeling a heightened sense of urgency. Eddie was a senior member and had served in the toughest fire-houses in the city. Something told me this was going to be it.

Everyone was on the rigs and out the door within twenty seconds. I was half-dressed in my protective gear when I first got on the rig. The call was less than half a mile away; I had to get dressed, and fast. I was panicking, frantically buckling my fire coat, putting on my hood, and trying to put on my air supply when the strap got stuck. *Oh man, I have to free myself. I could be tangled up and miss the job*, I thought. I was simultaneously swallowed up by the visions of the Trade Center and Michael's fate as he responded to his first fire. The lights and sirens catapulted me back into insanity. A few long seconds went by. I regained my composure and freed myself from the tangle. I was getting thrown around the rig every time we made a turn. I had the nozzle; I had to get dressed fast. People's lives and property depended on it.

Billy Dalton, a twenty-five-year veteran, assumed the position of backing me up, and Eddie, also a seasoned smoke eater, assumed the position of control. He was responsible for hooking up to the hydrant and supplying me with water. They were both sitting opposite me on the rig and kept telling me, "Relax, kid. Get dressed slowly. This could be your first job."

As we turned the corner, Lieutenant John Driscoll banged on the glass divider between the front and rear compartments of the rig, where we were sitting. "Guys, we got heavy smoke. We got a job."

This was it. I jumped off the rig and was greeted in the street with thick black smoke, reminding me of the smoke I witnessed on 9-11. I looked up at the second-floor windows, and the fire was roaring through them into the sky. My heart began to race; adrenaline kicked in. I was overcome with anxiety as I entered the smoky dwelling. Would I make it out unscathed? Would I disappoint the brothers? Was anyone trapped?

As I masked up and started my air supply, John Driscoll, with an experienced voice, told me, "It's going to be real hot up there. Relax, let your training kick in. We are in this together. When I open the door, don't open the line. We have to find the fire first."

We made our way up the century-old wooden staircase. With every tread as we ascended came a dismal creek, and in the back of my mind, I thought these stairs could give way. There was a lot of weight on them. I hoped they weren't compromised.

Driscoll controlled the door. "Are you ready, Joe?"

I cleared my throat, looked him dead in the eye, freed myself from any fears, and said, "Let's go." He opened the door. The heat was intense. We methodically went room to room, searching for the orange beast. There it was.

"Open up the line, Joe." I aggressively opened the hose and hit the fire. As soon as I did, we lost all visibility. I was holding onto the nozzle, trying to control the pressure. I pushed forward like a tornado, drenching the orange beast. I swept the floor as I advanced so we would not burn our knees.

Billy Dalton was backing me up, leaning his body onto mine, thrusting me forward. "Go get 'em, Joey, this is it," and he screamed with intensity as we were defeating the fire. It rolled over our heads onto the ceiling. I couldn't let it pass over and then get behind us; that's when firefighters become trapped. I aimed the nozzle above, knocking down the fire and its hopes of ever engulfing us. We pushed forward more, and just like that, it was out.

Shaken, soaked with sweat and water, I felt like I had achieved greatness. I did it. I immediately had a feeling that Michael was at my side, guiding me, that maybe those hadn't been Driscoll's words but Michael whispering in my ear.

I walked out of the charred dwelling into the street, holding the very nozzle that enabled me to extinguish the fire, as well as any chances of disaster that would have unfolded if we hadn't arrived.

I was greeted by the members of my company, who congratulated me on a good job, quickly followed by telling me of the tradition of taking them out for a beer after work to celebrate.

After my first fire, I found myself battling a newly acquired insatiability. I wanted to conquer any fears I had about working in Manhattan, the place that had claimed Michael's life, and to this day his final resting place.

I would have to fight an uphill battle against my wife and my parents. If I were to win, would I continue to follow Michael's footsteps and work at Ladder 11?

Chapter 10

See My Pain

Why couldn't anyone see the pain that had built a complex home in my soul? It should have been evident to everyone around me; they must have know that my old self was being held captive by the destructive, diabolical forces that overcame my subconscious.

The days were becoming so unbearable. I found myself regretting I wasn't killed on the eleventh alongside Michael. I was living my life, wishing the days would rapidly pass with hopes the pain would become manageable. Unfocused and unhappy in every aspect of life, I searched for what felt like eternity with no luck in finding a remedy to help me cope with the pain.

Taunted by the memories of the life I once took for granted, I was quickly self-destructing by the minute, with no hope in my future. I knew I was going to crash with tremendous force. I quickly had to save myself and those around me. If I couldn't, it would be disastrous.

I woke every day with hopes that this was all a bad dream, but within seconds I knew the grim details were a reality. I would lie in bed for hours, fantasizing that if there was a time machine that could take me back just a few years, I would pay any price just to take a voyage back before the eleventh and live a few more moments in the past. I would savor every second with Michael and my family, just to feel exhilarated once again. I yearned for the feeling I had grown accustomed to for the twenty-four years before that horrific day. God, I promised, if you could reverse this, I will never take life for granted again. I would become diligent and identify the life lessons that you wanted me to learn. Please help me; I don't think I can go on much longer like this.

I became extremely envious of schizophrenics. At least in some cases they were living a life of good and evil without being conscious of their other personality. On the other hand, while living with this unwanted personality, I was well aware of my old life. I remembered vividly what it was like to be happy and in control of a fantastic life. Now I suffered from the pain of not having it back and having my personality dominated by the post-traumatic stress that conquered my spirit. If it was my destiny to dwell with such pain and a heavy heart, why did God let me experience the great life I had and then take it all way? I would have rather not known beauty and happiness and just lived with pain from the beginning. At that point, would it have felt painful if I had known nothing else? At least I would have had innate coping mechanisms that would have helped me live a productive life in the face of stress, chaos, and pain.

Something in the pit of my stomach had tremendous control over every emotion I had left in my soul. It seemed like everything was slipping away from me in a whirlwind. I had an anger about me that was facilitating the destructive characteristics I acquired; to attach themselves to everyone I came in contact with, and begin to corrupt their lives as well.

My marriage with Maria was being contaminated by my new characteristics. I found myself constantly fighting with her. My pain and its byproducts were now bringing out the worst in her. I would go to work at the firehouse fighting with her. *Doesn't she realize I could die any second at work? I could end up like Michael in an instant. Why is she not forgiving me, why is she holding a grudge?* I would call her from work, trying to mend the situation, and when I got nowhere after reminding her of the dangers of my job, I resorted to my new training that was instilled in me by force, anger, and I would explode with rage.

This is the woman I love. Why couldn't she relate to what I was going through? Although she attended the memorial events that honored Mike and all those who were lost, part of me felt like she was doing it with hopes that it would come to an end. Believing she was just going through the motions infuriated me.

Day after day, my irrational state of mind would soon have rapid cell growth within the bodies of my friendships; it broke them down to a point of incapacitation, like stage-four cancers. I would constantly vent to them about the eleventh and my marital problems. When I didn't hear the responses I expected, I would become infuriated and radiate my negativity toward them.

After a while, my stories about the fighting with Maria and the eleventh became mundane in the eyes of friends closest to me. Maybe it was the cynical and repetitive nature of the substance behind the conversations I had with them. I don't know, but after a while, I began to see in their eyes that I was becoming a burden. They behaved as though they were listening just to pacify me; I know they weren't really listening anymore. My problems were slowly becoming theirs by force, and most of them seemed to shut me out in fear of having their positive outlook on life compromised.

I had no choice but to go to them. I wouldn't dare bring these issues up with my parents, sister, or grandmother. I knew they were taking it hard. In their eyes, I was the strength behind the family. Well, that was the aura I fraudulently depicted to them. God forbid they were having a good minute in their lives and I brought up my troubles. I would feel terribly guilty if I took that away from them, so I decided to hold it in or share it with my friends.

I was surrounded by negativity. Anyone who had good things going on in their lives started to stay far away from me. As a result, my friends became reluctant to speak of the great things that were going on in their lives because they didn't want me to feel out of place or get sucked back into the pain. So they simply started to recede from my life.

As I was getting closer to divorce with Maria, this really tested my relationships with my closest friends. I formed an aggression about myself that became uncontrollable. I became short-fused with everyone. I cross-examined every friend to find out Maria's whereabouts. The combination of the failing relationship and the tragedy intensified the pain and suffering I was enduring. How much worse could this become? How much more could I take?

I found myself starting new friendships with acquaintances and strangers. I went into a shell, as my problems intensified in my life. I believed a fresh start would be a temporary fix to my problem. Believe it or not, I believed if I didn't do this I would have no one in my life.

A few more months went by with my relationship with Maria quickly hitting rock bottom. I found myself in counseling once again, this time with her by my side. Who gets married in April and is in marriage counseling by the end of the summer? I couldn't even be happy in my marriage. We had originally scheduled our honeymoon for August 2002, roughly four months after we were married, because I was starting a new job and didn't want to ask for the time off right after I started.

By the time we embarked on our trip to the Atlantis resort in the Bahamas, our relationship was severely damaged. I recall her telling me that if we didn't experience an epiphany on this trip, we would have to separate. If I remember correctly, before the Fall of 2001, our relationship had been fun and exciting. Now it was an out-of-control runaway train, destined to be as big a disaster as the day Michael went missing.

The honeymoon was filled with controversy and turmoil. She told me she wanted a divorce; she wanted it over. She asked me, "When is all this 9-11 stuff going to be over? When is it my turn to be happy?" The instant she asked me this, I crumbled. The pain at that moment ripped through me like a can opener effortlessly cutting through tin, opening up my raw soul and setting whatever was left ablaze.

The questions would add fuel to an out-of-control fire within my soul. How could someone I love, who loved me, ask me that?

I was now heading home from the Bahamas with a familiar sense of uncertainty. I was at the absolute lowest point in my life. A brother was still missing, and a marriage was dissipating. Nothing was getting better; I began to question my very existence at this point. Would I ever be happy again? It seemed like my options were running out.

On December 31, 2002, Maria and I decided we'd had enough. She came to our apartment with her parents and neighbor and started to clean out her belongings. This process was anything but methodical. She was irrational, throwing things, screaming, and threatening me. At some point, her father, Lenny, also made it clear that I would have problems in the future. I quickly responded by informing him that my life was a tremendous problem, and that I had conditioned myself to dwell with the biggest demons that hell had released upon this earth. The relationship collapsed, as did everything else in this period of my life.

After she left, I changed the locks on the front door. I remember immediately feeling a sense of relief that this toxic relationship had been torn asunder. I then called a friend of Michael's, James Corson, and said I was getting divorced and I wanted to go out on the biggest night of the year, New Year's Eve. I had a thirst for starting 2003 in control of my life.

We headed to the city where we entered this party in VIP fashion. Dressed to kill, I roamed the party, seeking a new beginning in life. I actually didn't think of Maria once. Within minutes, I'd consumed large volumes of alcohol as the memories of the tragedy consumed my soul, intensely altering the stable way of life I once had. I immediately started to speak and reflect on the tragedy, thinking that if Mike were there, we would be controlling the atmosphere of this party. But he was not; he will never share a good time with me again, he is still buried in the rubble, missing. I was there, enjoying myself. What the fuck was wrong with me? I should be looking for him. Immense guilt started to seep into my brain. *Why am I here? Why is he gone? Why was I granted the privilege from God to survive and Mike wasn't?* He was a master of perfection, an old soul who was granted the gift of greatness in life, and I was not. *So why am I here?* It was time to pour out a little liquor for Mike and move on through the night. After all, I should be happy, and Maria was out of my life.

As the night intensified, so did the urge for me to control the night's destiny. I was hung up on consummating my new life. I wanted to take someone home to the apartment that my wife had stormed out of earlier and sleep with her. That night, a woman by the name of Ashley from California was in NYC for the festivities. She accompanied me home for a night and refreshed my memory of what it was to be adventurous and happy again, a feeling I had not had in more than a year.

As I woke up next to her, I distinctly remember hurrying her to leave the house with the same sense of urgency that civilians had when they left their desks that horrific September morning. Maybe Maria wanted to come home and reconcile. I had to get this woman out of my apartment. It was 9:00 AM; Maria might see her leave.

I never spoke to Ashley again. But I owe her a debt of gratitude for making me feel in control that night. I could see myself being addicted to the behavior I exhibited that New Year's Eve. Weeks passed, and I had not spoken to Maria; I was beginning to wonder if I would ever meet someone again.

Emptiness filled my soul every night when I went to bed. Even though we fought like Jews and Palestinians, at least I'd had someone next to me at night who was present when the nightmares took place.

I specifically remember two major friendships that were compromised. Both had maintained relationships with Maria. I couldn't believe that Brandon Carrabba, a friend I had known since I was in diapers was taking her to the movies with her friends. While the whole world was falling down around me, he decided he would console her, as she was going through the divorce process with me. Steven Sciarrino, someone who had always been there for me my whole life, the man that gave the speech in place of Michael at my wedding, who also grew up around the corner from me, was now getting on my fucking nerves. This was a guy who would walk through the fiery gates of hell with me if it were necessary, a guy who, in the past, put my best interests before his. Steve was someone who was a voice of reason when I was dealing with the catastrophes in my life, but that all went out the fucking window in my eyes. He was friends with Maria. He was trying to patch the relationship between us, but when it was evident that it would never happen, he backed off and still remained friends with her. I viewed him as a liaison between Maria and me. I used him as a source to retrieve information about her whereabouts, what she was up to, and if she was adjusting to life better than I. It might have not been right, but I didn't give a fuck; this was about me now, and it was making me happy. After a while, I began to believe Steve and Brandon were in cahoots with Maria, that possibly one of them could have been starting a relationship with her.

Before the eleventh, I would have never had these heinous thoughts. But now, this uncontrollable persona was polluting my mind with these scenarios.

It was only a matter of time before I found a way to find fault even in the person who was by my side during the eleventh: Jerome. At some point, I felt he had abandoned me for his new girlfriend.

Jealousy was even consuming my mind with relationships I had with my guy friends. What the fuck was going on with me?

One relationship I totally destroyed simply because I lost touch when he needed me most, which, by the way, was his entire time after the eleventh, was someone Mike and I were very close to: Chris Vallone. A great friend and great fishing buddy, he basically told me he couldn't deal with my shit anymore and ended our relationship, just as one flips a light switch.

To add insult to injury, my family, especially my closest cousins, didn't want anything to do with my aggressive behavior. They thought I was rough and rigid when I was in their presence.

Fuck everyone was the way I felt as I walked the earth. Nothing or no one knew what I was going through. I feared getting tired at night; I fought to keep my eyes open because I feared falling asleep, knowing the nightmares would torture me. I was living in a horror movie with no end in sight! Couldn't anyone see my pain?

Chapter 11

Blood Brother

A few months after the eleventh, my mother, Linda, read a *New York Post* article. It stated that firefighters who donated blood may still have their blood preserved. The blood was donated to the National Marrow Donor program, set up to screen donors' blood to see if they are compatible to help someone who may have leukemia or other life-threatening diseases.

Sure enough, after I investigated, Michael had donated blood, and they had it. I wanted to arrange to take possession of it. This was the only viable piece of him to be recovered to date. My mother didn't want to obtain it. She told me, "Joey, it's like we are giving up bringing him home. It's only been a few months; I still have hope, and I can't give up on my baby." My reasoning behind taking it was because I believed they would never find him. I didn't want to tell my mother that, though. Hope was the only thing motivating her to go on, and I didn't want to take that away from her.

A few more months went by. I persistently wanted to lay him to rest. His remains still hadn't been recovered. Nothing to that point had been identified. It was tearing my heart out more and more as the days went on. My mother still didn't want to move forward on it; she broke down in front of me as we were discussing it. "What are we going to do, lay his blood to rest? And what if they find more, what will we do then? Dig up his grave and disturb his resting place? I am not ready for this yet." I respected her wishes at that moment.

It was now the middle of March 2003, and they were getting ready to cart out the last piece of debris from the site. It was a tremendous steel cross, with distinguishable markings of remembrance on it. Seventeen months had passed, and the recovery and cleanup had come to an end. He still wasn't recovered. Not one goddamn remnant of his existence. That day was one of the worst days since the eleventh. We all had some type of hope that he would be returned home to us. That day, I knew it was over. My brother Michael had been turned to dust. He disappeared that day, wiped off the face of the earth, just like that. There was no equipment, tools, or bunker gear with his name on it, nothing. There was no body matter left, nothing to say he was here on planet earth except that vial of blood. If we didn't collect the vial, he would never be brought home to us.

It was halfway through May of 2003 and still no remains. DNA testing had been put on hold, and technology must advance before those severely decomposed remains could be further examined. One day when I came home from a tour at the firehouse, around 1000 hours, my mother was waiting for me on the steps of her house. She looked me in the eye and told me to give her a hug. "I am ready. I need you to set up the arrangements."

Before I could pick up the blood, I had to make arrangements with the fire and police departments. We organized a helicopter flyover, as well as all the ceremonial bells and whistles. If we were finally going to lay him to rest, almost two years later, we had to do it in a big way. All members of the departments were notified, up to the rank of commissioner and the mayor himself, Michael Bloomberg.

We wanted to have the service the week before Memorial Day in May. But we had hit an unexpected roadblock. Our house of worship, Michael's parish, Our Lady Star of the Sea Church, would not let us have the service. Actually, they would, but we were not allowed to bring Michael's casket into the church. Their reasoning for that was that there was no body in the casket. This infuriated my family. They wanted us to leave the casket guarded outside the church doors while the precession went on. They must have been kidding me. My mother, once again, was crumbling to pieces. This woman couldn't even lay her son to rest without resistance.

With all the suns and moons aligned for the burial arrangements besides the church, I decided to reach out to the ceremony unit within the fire department. Once they got wind of this preposterous scenario, some phone calls were made to the church, possibly the archdiocese of New York, and probably the press, and within one day, we had overturned the church's ruling on Michael's casket. Whoever made it happen, my family owes you a debt of gratitude.

The date was set for Saturday, June 7, 2003. All the preparation had been done except picking up the vial of his blood. I arranged to pick it up; my mother didn't have the strength to participate in the process. I wanted someone who not only knew Mike to ride with me to get it but who had experienced that day with me: my police partner, Jerome Crimi. We were picked up at my home in a Fire Department Family Assistance vehicle and slowly escorted to Manhattan, where we had to claim his blood. As we exited the tunnel and passed Ground Zero, I was slowly sucked into a flashback of that morning. I smelled the burning debris, tasted the contaminated air as if I were inhaling it, and heard those pass alarms again. I was momentarily back on the battlefield as I was that morning. I felt myself once again running from the collapsing buildings, thinking this was war. Am I ever going to be able to live a normal life, in control of at least one thing, my emotions?

I snapped totally out of it when we walked into the facility. I thought, *Is this really how he is going to be recovered? Thank God he donated this blood, because if he hadn't, we would never have any piece of physical closure.*

There it was. A staff member of the facility presented it to me. Entombed in a leather box, I slowly opened it. I started to sweat, and this was it: the only physical makeup on this planet of Mike was there in my hand. It was on dry ice, wrapped tightly around with a red bow. This blood once ran through his heart, and I was now holding it, with the mission of safely transporting it for his proper burial. Our family, the city, and the nation as a whole owed it to him to carry out this mission.

I slept right next to the freezer that night; I guarded his remains from everything from a power outage to an intruder. I lay awake that night, reflecting on our childhood, our friendship, and, of course, trying to piece together the events of that morning as they unfolded right before his eyes. I wondered what he thought, if he had been scared, if he knew this was his time to go, and if he thought he would make it out alive.

While asleep on the eve of his burial, I had an interesting visit. I had a dream of Michael. Dressed all in white, he looked magnificent. He thanked me for bringing him home to momma. He was worried about her the most. I woke feeling bringing him home not only satisfied us but him as well.

The next morning, we arrived bright and early at the funeral parlor. This was going to be the place we said our last goodbyes privately, as a family. His casket lay there, open. It was beautiful, blue and brushed nickel, his favorite color. The casket was empty except for a photo of him in his bunker gear at the head of the casket. We each brought a few items along with us to place in the casket before his blood was put inside. We each read a letter to him that would be placed in the casket. We didn't make it one sentence into the first letter, read by my father, before we all went to pieces. The most painful of all though was my mother's letter. I can still see her sobbing and reading as the mascara she was wearing dripped onto her lapel. It was something I would not wish on anyone. It had been almost two years, and the pain was still unbearable. The thought of him vanishing was unbelievable. We then methodically placed his dress uniform from the FDNY in the casket. It was placed as if he were lying in it, everything from the patent leather dress shoes placed at the bottom to the cap and badge forever placed on the top of the casket. His uniform shirt, pants, and belt were laid carefully in their respective places. Photos and memorabilia were next. Anything that brought joy to him and reminded us of his life on earth was painfully placed in the casket. Hockey sticks, his Little League all-star hat, and glove that he wore in the Little League World Series would be forever with his blood.

I slowly closed the casket. We were ready. If closure wouldn't happen naturally, I would control it by laying his blood and artifacts to rest.

More than ten thousand people showed up. Members of service from the city and as far away as California and Boston flew in for this ceremony. Civilians packed the church, the grass, the property, and the streets, all the way to the train station. Speakers were set up so the people who weren't fortunate enough to get a seat in the church could hear the service.

As we got out of the limousine, we were greeted by those same haunting bagpipes, a symphony that reminded me of the presence of death and the grim reaper. Simultaneously, the bells rang to signify a fallen comrade in the line of duty. They were followed by a loud voice, "Attention, order arms." Everyone saluted the casket. Slowly, the fire department pallbearers walked the casket into the church. From a distance, you heard the spinning rotors of the two police department helicopters slowly approaching. The sound intensified as they got closer. They were flying no higher than the power lines in front of the church as they passed overhead. I felt as if a door had been closed forever. This was really it. It started to sink in that very moment that he was gone forever.

As he gave his emotional eulogy about Michael, Mayor Bloomberg took a stance for the first time on the controversial debate whether emergency personnel who responded and gave their lives on 9-11 deserved a separate memorial than those of civilian casualties. "I personally believe the memorial at the World Trade Center site must provide recognition to firefighters, police officers, and EMTs, who like Michael, fell saving the lives of others. We must ensure that the future generations will be able to read their names, know what they did, appreciate their heroism, be inspired by their sacrifice, and ensure they are designated as role models for the next generation who will protect us."

Headlines the next day in the *Daily News* read, "Mike Stirs 9/11 Memorial Feud." This was the first time any politician had taken a stance on what they sincerely believed about the degree of separation at the memorial site. I respected his courage for making it known that day. It was added inspiration that my family, and the families of all the rescue workers who fell that day needed to hear to ensure that their sacrifices would forever be recognized. The media pelted Bloomberg, stating that the stance he took at the funeral would influence the thirteen-member panel who would vote on the issue. He fired back, saying those members are independent people, capable of making their decisions based on what they believe.

We finally had a piece of Michael recovered and laid to rest. This served as a piece of closure, which we needed at this moment in our lives. I felt my future trips to the cemetery wouldn't be to visit a tombstone that sat on virgin ground but to visit the final resting place of America's youngest hero on 9-11, my brother Michael Cammarata.

Blood Brother
Michael coming home from the fire academy on the first day.

Chapter 12

Looking Back

The journey through the first twenty-four years of my life was a blessed one. It was a privilege for anyone to experience any piece of Michael. I was the luckiest person on the earth. I had the tightest bond with him, something no cowardly terrorist could strip from me.

Best friends from the moment he was born, there was nothing we wouldn't do for each other. There will always be a vacancy for a best friend in my life; this is a spot that could never be filled by anyone else. The only things that occupy it now are vivid memories from our childhood until the eleventh. Since then, many things have triggered me to reflect on memories of Michael. It can be anything from cologne that he wore to the car he drove past me to a schoolyard where we played when we were children.

Best friends
Me, Michael, and my Poppy: Sgt Major George Warren, U.S. Army

Living with the constant reminders of him was a double-edged sword. One part of me never wanted the triggers to stop, because I was terrified that his memory would fade. But the other part of me wanted time, time not to think of the tragedy and to move closer to closure.

My earliest memories of him were when we were two and three years old, dressing up as firefighters from head to toe, including fire engine underwear; I kid you not.

Being that we were only fifteen months apart and one grade difference in school, we had all the same friends. This brought us even closer than a typical sibling relationship.

There was a seven to eight year difference in age between Kim, our sister, and us. To her, we were her pesky little brothers; to us, she was an older sister we both looked up to.

The days of playing in the schoolyard of our grade school, P.S. 35 in Staten Island, New York, are what taught us how to forge strong relationships with our peers and experience healthy competition. Whether it was choosing teams to play baseball, basketball, or handball, there was always competition and always heated games. But at the end of the day, we all were best of friends.

Rob Hirsch, Todd Dana, Michael Parisi, Thomas Arlotta, Nicholas Farina: those were just a bunch of friends we would spend all day with, competing in schoolyard games that were like the World Series or Super Bowl to us.

Michael was a phenomenal athlete since the day he started playing sports. He wanted, at minimum, to up his skill level to the next age group, because I was always playing on a team or a division that was one year ahead of him. He wouldn't be second fiddle to anyone or anything.

We started to play ice hockey at the ages of six and seven. This occupied our winters, and our springs and summers were occupied by Little League.

In 1988, my parents decided to build a home on the South Shore of the island. This meant Mike and I were going to have to make new friends in our new neighborhood. My cousins, Nicky and Carolyn Jane, and friends Brandon and Vince, relocated from

Brooklyn and were living only a few short streets from my new home. So the transition into the new neighborhood was easier.

As the house was being built on Kingdom Avenue, Mike and I noticed at least fifteen kids playing different sports in the street: roller hockey, baseball, basketball, and football. We wanted to introduce ourselves, but I felt intimidated at first.

Then we noticed a large group of kids were playing roller hockey with these bright orange nets made of plumbing pipe and orange construction netting. It just so happened that we conveniently had our roller blades, hockey sticks, and gloves with us.

We skated toward the makeshift street arena, wearing our bright blue roller blades, which were only available by order from Canada. Since they weren't available in the United States yet, you can imagine the looks on the faces of those kids. To them, we looked like aliens who had landed in the middle of their hockey game. Mike and I couldn't help but look at each other, as we both noticed that some of the guys were wearing figure skates—some black, some even white—like they had stolen them out of their sisters' closets.

We introduced ourselves and were greeted by Steven Sciarrino; the Cozetto brothers, Anthony and Mike; Chris and Mike D'Gaeta; Brian Burns; John and Scott Nitti; and a few other kids who didn't actually live on the block. An instantaneous bond with these guys was formed.

Stickball, baseball, handball, football, manhunt, Marco Polo and volleyball in the pool, and video games were a few things that we immediately started doing with our new friends.

A few weeks later, we met Kevin Griswold and Chris Vallone, two more friends we would become very close with over time.

Looking Back
Back row: L→R: Mike Degaeta, Mike Cozzetto, Chris Vallone
Center: Mike Cammarata, Anthony Lamantia
Bottom: L→R: Brandon Carrabba, Anthony Cozzetto, Joseph Cammarata

Chris, Mike, and I would have our daily fishing excursions to various bodies of water. Believe it or not, there was even competition in that, too. We would spend every vacant summer day riding on New York City buses and trains with our tackle boxes, fishing poles, and stinky bait heading to our favorite fishing holes. We even envisioned ourselves becoming professional anglers and possibly having our very own sponsored fishing show on the sports channel.

Mike's competitive attitude while playing sports landed him on several all-star teams in hockey and baseball. One team that brought copious memories was the 1991 South Shore Little League team that made their journey defeating all teams on the island, the city, the state, and on the east coast to advance to the Little League World Series.

He was also a standout hockey player. By the time we reached the high school varsity level in the early 1990s, he was leading the team, the Tottenville Pirates, to the playoffs. Rookie of the year, MVP, and best defenseman were all awards he racked up over the years.

I was playing on the right side, and he was playing on the left. We were a defensive team that worked well together because we were blood. We had played together since we were children and instinctively knew what each others' next moves were going to be. We protected each other on the ice with the same care as we did off the ice. Our brotherhood was growing stronger each and every day. He was a true leader; that's the reason he became an assistant captain, and then captain the following year. I was the older brother but was looking to my younger brother for leadership on and off the ice.

By the time Mike was a senior, he was still playing defense but was actually in contention for the scoring title midway through the season. In the press, there was a lot of talk that he would fizzle out by the end of the year. The press must have been relying on the history that no other defensemen in New York Ice Hockey Association history had ever accomplished that feat.

It was down to the last game. Mike was contending against two Farrell Lions players, Chris Baboulis and Lou Weber, for the scoring title. They had played their last game the night before. Mike needed three goals and two assists to pull off history. The pressure must have been enormous, but I remember him telling me that he was just going out there to play hockey.

The stands were loaded with fans, press, and college scouts, all there to witness the possibility of the first defenseman to win the scoring title.

By the third period, Mike only had one point; he knocked out an assist. They were losing 4–1. With ten minutes left, he assisted another goal, which made it 4–2. There were five minutes left. He skated past two forwards and only had to beat one defenseman. He faked left, accelerated right, and beat the goalie in the upper right corner. It was now 4–3. Three minutes remained, and the play had moved into the oppositions offensive zone. I was sitting in the stands in disbelief. *He is gonna pull this off, I know it.* Paul DiChristina had the puck down low. Mike left the blue line and headed to the net full speed. Paulie fired the puck right on Mike's stick. Mike one-timed it right through the goalies legs. Goal, 4–4, tie game.

Time expired; they were now heading to overtime. Another fifteen minutes passed on the clock. The other team had the pressure on the Pirates in their defensive zone. The anxiety was building in the arena; the Pirates needed the game to ensure a playoff berth, plus the crowd wanted to witness history. John Kelly, the Pirates' goalie, made a phenomenal kick save; the puck ricocheted into the corner.

Mike picked it up behind the goal line, skated behind the net, and turned toward center ice. Then the legs kicked in, and he started to blow by the opponents like they were orange cones standing still. It was just him and the goalie. Who will it be? Mike dips left, shoots high right. Everything was in slow motion, the puck was stopped by the fabric netting tightly secured to the red iron piping, while a full green Gatorade bottle lying on the top of the net was thrown in the air and landed on the ice. Score! All I remember is the crowd going nuts. They did it, the Pirates moved to the playoffs, and Mike made history. He was the first defenseman ever to win the scoring title.

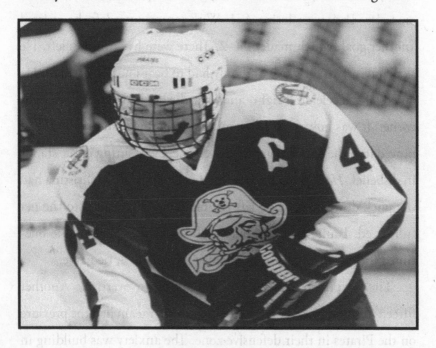

MVP
Mike, senior year of high school

He continued his studies at Wagner College and played hockey for the school. He became rookie of the year his freshman year, and sophomore and junior years he secured MVP status.

His charisma on the ice also carried with him off the ice. He earned the nickname Face because of his movie-star good looks and his smooth character with the ladies.

We went on several vacations together. First was Miami and then Cancun. We had an amazing time. He would always go the extra mile, spend more money, pull the most out of his time on the trip, because he may have known his life was going to be cut short.

He was a man of a million sneakers, I swear. He loved his Nike sneakers. He kept them organized in his closets like soldiers marching in a parade. He had at least forty pairs, and they were all in mint condition.

He wore the most amazing clothes. I found myself going to him on several occasions for fashion advice, as well as advice about different life obstacles.

He was the biggest ball breaker. Being as good-looking as he was, I sometimes think it went to his head. He thought he was a comedian, always making jokes at my expense. Sometimes I felt like I was the little brother. I was the older brother who looked up to him.

I love retreating into the past and reliving my childhood memories of him and the lifelong bond that still lives on in my heart.

Mike, I love you, miss you, and will forever remember the bond we had. You truly were and continue to be a mentor in my life. Until we meet again, brother.

The Face's Crew
Our entire crew from our college days in Cancun, Mexico

Old Friends
Mike, Chris, Brandon, and Me

The Crew
L→R Joe Profeta, Steve Sciarrino, me, Mike, Frank Iervasi

Three's Company
L→R Me, Kim, and Mike

Cancun 2000
Me, Mike partying in Cancun 2000

World Series 1991
Mike Playing right field representing the East in the 1991 Little League World Series

Chapter 13

Hometown Hero

It was a frigid January day in 2002. As the winter months followed the tragedy, our hopes of bringing Michael home became frozen in time. We were going through a rough period in our lives as a family, my mother in particular. She still had not recovered her baby, Michael, had never had the opportunity to kiss his face one more time before he was buried. She also found herself grappling with me, trying to convince me with all her might not to join the FDNY on January 14, 2002.

Leaving that cold morning of January 14, 2002, to be sworn in as one of New York's Bravest was bittersweet. I knew I was tearing my mother's heart out by moving forward with my plans to be a firefighter, and I was fulfilling a dream I had but without Michael. My mother came to realize quickly that standing in the way of her son's dream would not make her happy either. As I walked out the door to be sworn in, she told me, "Joe, I always want you to remember Michael is watching over you. Good luck today. I love you."

When I arrived back home later that afternoon, my mother answered the door with a look of happiness in her eyes that I had not seen since before September 11, 2001. She told me Michael would receive Little League Baseball's highest honor. He was going to be forever enshrined into the Hall of Excellence. She told me she had received a phone call from the president and CEO of Little League Baseball, Stephen D. Keener. He expressed his condolences and told her that Little League Baseball across the globe wanted to participate and help fulfill one of Michael last requests, to "Make my spirit live on." He also informed us that Michael was going to be the first posthumous recipient of this honor in the history of Little League Baseball.

Mr. Keener also informed us Michael was the inspiration behind the newly formed Little League initiative, Honoring Our Hometown Heroes. This initiative was designed so that Little League participants would honor, recognize, and aspire to be like the local heroes who protect them as well as the heroes who gave their lives on the morning of September 11, 2001. A press release was in the works, and the whole world would soon learn officially about the phenomenal person Michael was and about the great honor he would receive.

My mother also told me another astonishing fact: being enshrined with Michael on the same day was former mayor Rudy

Giuliani, "America's mayor," a personal hero of mine since before the attacks on September 11. The feeling that very moment was overwhelming. I immediately ran to the computer, fired it up, and researched the Web to see who was enshrined before him. And there it was: George W. Bush, the president of the United States of America. This was amazing.

As the months went by, the anticipation of returning to Williamsport built up. Except this time, we weren't going to support Michael competing, representing the East as he did in the 1991 Little League World Series, but to receive the highest honor Little League Baseball awarded. I counted down the time until the fifty-sixth annual Little League World Series that was going to be held in August 2002.

Word started to spread like wildfire. Michael, again, was making the headlines as a result of the upcoming honor that was going to be presented to him posthumously. As much publicity and recognition as he was getting, it would have satisfied me a hell of a lot more if he had survived that day and was able to accept this award as a result of his heroic efforts. The feeling was bittersweet; he was gone and would never be seen again, but he would live through every Little Leaguer who plays the sport.

August arrived. It was time to head up to the headquarters of Little League Baseball. The faculty treated us as if we were royalty. They sat us down and explained the agenda for the weekend and how everything would be scheduled. Then they took us to the Hall of Excellence. As I walked up to view the inductees, I was star-struck by my own brother's monument nestled between another hero of mine, Rudy Giuliani, and George Bush. He was going to be immortalized forever alongside some of the most influential people who have ever existed on this planet. This feeling could be compared to nothing I had ever experienced in my lifetime. It was literally breathtaking.

His brightly lit plaque stood out like a beacon of light among the rest for a few reasons. He was the youngest and the only one who had been enshrined wearing firefighter gear. Instantaneously, anyone who would look at this display without reading the verbiage would know he had given his life in the line of duty on September 11, 2001.

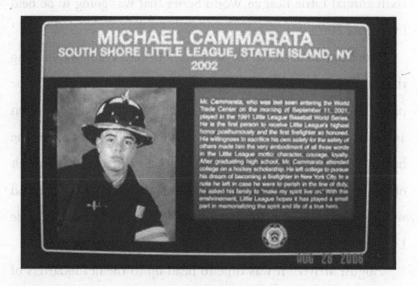

World Series Hall of Excellence Enshrinement

The plaque, inscribed *Michael Cammarata—2002* (the year he was inducted), read: "Michael Cammarata, who was last seen rushing into the World Trade Center on the morning of Sept. 11,

2001, played in the 1991 Little League Baseball World Series for the South Shore Little League of Staten Island, N.Y. He is the first person to receive Little League's highest honor posthumously and the first firefighter so honored. His willingness to sacrifice his own safety for the safety of others made him the very embodiment of all three words in the Little League motto: character, courage, and loyalty. After graduating high school, Mr. Cammarata attended college on a hockey scholarship. He left college to pursue his dream of becoming a firefighter in New York City. In a note he left in case he were to perish in the line of duty, he asked his family to 'Make his spirit live on.' Little League hopes it has played a small part in memorializing the spirit and life of a true hero."

After my mother, father, sister, and I read this, we broke down in tears. I became so choked up I had to step out of the room and collect myself. This was so amazing; every Little Leaguer who visits this museum will know about Mike. To date, this clearly was the biggest honor he had received.

The day after was the official induction on the field before the U.S. Championship game. Rudy Giuliani was unable to attend the service that day, but he wrote a letter that was read in front of the crowd. He noted, "I am honored to be selected to be a member of the Hall of Excellence, along with a great hero like Michael Cammarata." This was another inspirational part Mr. Giuliani has played in our lives.

It was now my turn to say a few words about what this honor meant to our family and what Michael would say if he were there.

I was very nervous. Although I had spoken publicly about Michael on numerous occasions, I had never spoken in front of thirty-five thousand people at one time. Yeah, thirty-five thousand people attended the U.S. Championship game at the Little League World Series. A podium was set directly on the pitcher's mound. My whole family walked out and was greeted by Mr. Keener. He introduced us as the family of Michael Cammarata and spoke a few moments about Michael. My mother immediately went to tears in front of the crowd. It was now my turn to speak. I wanted the full-capacity crowd to really get to know who Michael was in my speech. I also spoke about the tremendous honor it was for him to be immortalized in the baseball world. When I was finished with my speech, there were thirty-five thousand people standing on their feet, chanting, "USA, USA, USA," as the F51 fighter pilots roared overhead. It was at that very point I knew Michael and what he had done that day would never be forgotten.

There had only been twenty-eight people inducted before Michael. Aside from Rudy and George Bush, some other recognizable inductees were:

Kevin Costner 2000

Tony Dungy 1998

Bruce Springsteen 1997

Cal Ripken Jr. 1997

Dale Murphy 1995

Kareem Abdul-Jabbar 1992

Nolan Ryan 1991

Mike Schmidt 1991

Tom Selleck 1991

Vice president Dan Quayle 1990

Senator Bill Bradley 1989

Tom Seaver 1991

Other enshrines consisted of entrepreneurs, astronauts, doctors, scientists, and other influential role models children who play Little League Baseball should aspire to be like one day.

With the fifth anniversary of one of the darkest days approaching fast, we were once again contacted by the headquarters of Little League Baseball. They wanted to commemorate him once again, and this time they wanted to permanently affix his number 11 on the right-field wall, where he played, to pay tribute to sacrifices he made that day. This was amazing. Five years ago, they immortalized his very soul, preserved the history of his existence so everyone would know him. Now they wanted to honor him on the very field where he played, at the exact position that he played. This is world-class recognition.

Once again, we walked onto the field and experienced how the foundation of America's pastime is honoring Mike again. It was amazing. His number was forever affixed to the position he played in right field in Howard J. Lamade Stadium. Stephen Keener spoke again to the fans in attendance at the U.S. Championship game and told them, "In the years to come, people will ask, 'What is the number 11 in right field for?' We will be able to tell them the story of a Little Leaguer who became a true hero for all of us." He added,

"That the spirit of Michael Cammarata will forever roam in right field in Howard J. Lamade Stadium."

Once again, the Little League Baseball organization treated us like family. They once again expressed their gratitude toward the sacrifices Michael made for America. The compassion and respect these people have showed us has played an instrumental role in our recovery from this tragedy. We will forever be grateful, as we know Michael is as he looks down on these recognitions of his soul. Thank you, Little League Baseball, for forever immortalizing my brother, my hero, Michael Cammarata.

Batting
Mike batting in the 1991 Little League World Series

Right Field
*Mike playing right field at the 1991 Little League World
Series*

His Retired Number
This is his number, forever affixed to the right-field wall at the Little League World Series

Chapter 14
Facing My Fears

The whole time I was stationed in Staten Island, New York, at Engine Company 157, I had a burning desire to transfer to a firehouse in Manhattan, with the intention of conquering any fear I had about working in the borough of the City of New York that prematurely claimed the life of my brother.

It was a process that was strategically thought out. Although I came to the conclusion it was something I wanted to do, I had one problem: explaining to my parents, especially my mother, that this was what I wanted to do.

One day I had a long conversation with her, sitting on the stone planters that she built in the lush garden she'd planted. I explained to her that Michael started a mission in 2001, and it had become my duty since he passed on to carry out that mission. At first she was against it, but I pressed on. I told her what I truly felt, how facing this fear, because it truly was a fear, would mold me into a man. I expressed that transferring to Manhattan would serve as a piece of closure, something I desperately needed in my life at that time. I assured her the members of the Manhattan fire companies had elite training and that the department, although protocol hadn't been changed, has become more cautious in the face of catastrophe. I also reminded her that the job had been proven to be deadly, no matter what region of the city you work in.

I don't know if she gave me her blessing because of my sincerity in facing a fear that haunted me, or if she let me make my own decision without resistance because she didn't want to play a part in picking my poison.

I chose Engine Company 54, Ladder 4 for several reasons. First and foremost, it was located in Midtown, Eighth Avenue and Forty-eighth Street, in the center of it all, around the corner from Times Square. Second, I was familiar with one of its members, someone I had become very close with over the last two years, Tommy Hunt, my carpool buddy and academy friend. Last, they lost fifteen members on the eleventh, the most of any company on the job. This company, which suffered the largest numerical loss, would confirm that my fears had been faced and dealt with.

When I arrived at the house to introduce myself before my first tour of duty, I walked into the kitchen to find the whole company preparing lunch at the table. I noticed one off-duty member, in civilian clothes, who resembled the actor Ryan Philippe. He had blonde hair, blue eyes, and an attitude about his face as he sat slouched in the chair. I introduced myself to the entire company and noticed he was the only one who didn't acknowledge my existence. He was about my age. I had a feeling he was putting on a cocky front, because he might have felt threatened. But I knew he would eventually come around.

Working with my buddy Tommy Hunt at the center of the universe was immeasurable. After work, we would go out to the local bars and lounges to unwind and meet interesting people. I was single at the time, recently divorced, and found that my life was starting to become adventurous again.

The Pride of Midtown
A picture of me proudly displaying my new company pride at Engine 54

We ran like crazy at work. Our company did almost five thousand calls a year. I felt like I was really learning the job, as well as learning about myself. I became extremely close with some of the members of the company, including Pat Moore, that wiseass who didn't say hello to me the first day. Not only were we becoming close in the firehouse, risking our lives together at work, we became dependant on each other on the fire floor.

As new probies came in, we all ragged on the new guys, initiating them as they entered our internal firehouse brotherhood. One probie in particular, Freddie Martinez, a firefighter and freelance actor on the side, fit into our little clique immediately. He was as smooth with the ladies as a baby's bare ass. He liked to party and was always down for action, whether it was fighting a fire, traveling to Miami with me, Tommy, and Pat, or going to the Copacabana and trying to educate us on how to salsa properly.

Every time the tone alarms went off and announced fire at a certain address in the concrete jungle known as Manhattan, and I suited up with my pals and jumped on the rig, I had an overwhelming feeling that Michael was riding along with me, suited up, ensuring my safety.

These guys I met in the city weren't only my coworkers or best friends; they were my mentors, teaching me how to live my life again. They were right by my side the whole time I was facing my fears, and for that, I am grateful.

FDNY Brothers
Pat Moore and me in the firehouse after a call

Miami Nights
Tommy hunt on the left, me, and Pat Moore in a Miami club

Chapter 15

Becoming an Executor

"This life-altering event has held me down long enough" was a familiar statement I have told many people. It was supposed to serve as a catapult, springing me back into control of my life. It became a repetitive phrase that didn't have any validation to it. I couldn't seem to escape the black hole of depression I was living in and seize my life back. Motivation was nonexistent.

I knew losing Michael in the fashion that we did could incapacitate me from ever achieving my goals in life. I had to break free from those forces and get back on my feet again. I had one life, and at any second, it could be taken from me. This life had taken enough from me; I had to escape from these emotional restraints now. The only thing was, I wouldn't be able to do this alone.

It was a beautiful spring Friday in 2004. I was on the freeway, about to enter the Brooklyn Battery Tunnel. I was heading to the city for a tour of duty at my firehouse in midtown Manhattan when I decided to call my old martial arts instructor, whom I trained with from 1996 to 1999. I hadn't spoke to him since our school was divided five years earlier. Hell, I wasn't even sure he was going to entertain the request I had of him, but I tried anyway.

He was about nine years older, invincible in his fighting stature as well as the character he walked the earth with. He was just the discipline I needed desperately in my life right then. Motivational from every life aspect, he had a commanding way about him that would push you to overcome any life challenge in your way. I hadn't seen him since right before my black belt grading in March of 1999. I was nervous to see if he would answer my call.

We never had any bad blood between us. In fact, if I remember correctly, he encouraged the students to stay with the instructors who were running the school when the split took place. I honored his request and hadn't seen or heard from him since.

With my cold and clammy hands, I scrolled through my phone until I arrived at his name. I must have stared at it a good thirty seconds while sitting in traffic before I pushed send. I thought, *If I want to rid myself of the reluctant lifestyle I have been living the last three years, I'd better get my nuts up and just hit the send button.*

I was caught at a crossroads. I contemplated pushing the send button. This was potentially something that could change my life. Little did I know pushing the send button on my phone that beautiful day was going to change my life for an eternity. This would become the first step to my achieving greatness in this world, the first step to becoming an executor.

As I engaged the send button, the screen immediately read, "Calling Frank Barone." With no turning back, I nervously tried to rehearse the dialogue I was going to start with. Then a robust, commanding voice stated, "This is Frank." Clearing my throat, I said, "Frank, this is Joe Cammarata, an old student from your New Dorp Karate School. I went up the ranks under you just about a month before I was graded for black belt. Do you remember me?" Without hesitation he answered, "Of course I do. How are you and your family doing? I heard about your brother."

I told him not so well and that was one of the reasons I was calling him. I wanted to get my life back; I wanted to train with him again. If anyone was going to get me motivated again and focused, it was going to be him.

He welcomed my request with open arms. "Be at my house 5:00 AM this Sunday. Does that work for you?" Hesitant in my thoughts, also thinking that there was something wrong with this guy, I told him to e-mail his address and I would see him at 5:00 AM sharp.

As I waited for his e-mail, I was hoping he would reconsider the start time of the training and maybe push it back to a reasonable time of 10:00 AM. Literally a minute later, I received a text message with his address and the time of 5:00 AM, followed by the words in full capital letters, "DON'T BE LATE."

What the hell did I get myself into? Not only is this guy a top martial artist, dangerous as a hired assassin, he wants to roll with me before the roosters wake up. I hoped I wouldn't regret this.

That Saturday night, I set my alarm for 4 AM. I wanted to take a cold shower to wake myself up, as well as heighten my instincts, something necessary at a high level of fighting. I grabbed my dormant American Vadha Kempo karate duffel bag and my flashlight and headed to the car.

I drove the almost eight miles to his house without seeing the existence of one motorist or civilian roaming the streets. I passed several bakeries that hadn't even turned on their lights yet to start baking for their biggest day of the week. This was borderline psychotic!

I turned down Oakley Drive and onto Cubberly Lane; I was searching for house #31. Parking was scarce, so I took the only spot on the block, way before his home. Dark is an understatement; all the houses had every single light out. How the hell was I going to read the addresses? I wasn't about to whip out that flashlight. People might think I was a prowler at that wee hour.

I gently closed my car door; I didn't want to wake anyone. It was 4:45 AM. I slowly headed down the dark street toward what I believed to be the direction I needed to be heading. The thumping of my footsteps was the only thing I believed you could hear for miles—until I heard a crisp sound from a few hundred yards away. As I got closer, it sound like someone or something exhaling. I thought, *This can't be. No one in the borough is up yet except me.*

As I walked further down the street, I heard that sound of alleged exhalation intensify. I started to search for its whereabouts. I was curious to see what was out there. Could it be a wild animal of some sort, or a loose pit bull? I scanned the area frantically, trying to identify the source of this sound. Then I locked in; my eyes came into focus. The sound was coming from the porch of what seemed to be a dwelling that resembled an old English Tudor home. I took two more steps, stopped, and then forced my eyes to focus on the being creating erratic sound and motion. It was a tall, dark shadow, aggressively and rapidly moving in a contained area. I couldn't believe it. It was Frank.

He was warming up. He looked like he was sparring someone right there on his steps. *This guy has to be kidding me.*

We picked up where we left off. The student-mentor relationship had been frozen in time for the past five years and had thawed from the phone call until now. I knew I had to step up my game if I was going to continue training with him.

The first words out of his mouth after the session was done were, "You know I have to grade you for black belt, right?" I told him I had a certificate with me from my previous grading instructor, as well as one from the founder of the style, John Salvaggio, a grandmaster who holds the rank of tenth degree. I explained to him that I had the six-hour grading videotaped and had sent down to Florida for Salveggio's examination and certification. He didn't care. Frank told me I should do well then when he grades me. If I wanted to be in his circle of training, trust, and black belts, he would have to grade me his way; he wanted to validate my skills.

He put me on a schedule of training three to four times weekly, at these early hours, to prepare me for my grading. Every time I arrived at his house at 5:00 AM, he was waiting for me in the same spot, shadowboxing.

He was testing my will to commit to something. He wanted to see if I was committed with the same intensity as I had been the first day we trained months earlier.

That is what I needed at that time to get my life back on track. The ability to stick to a strict discipline no matter how intense the conditions were became my top priority. I had to shake the unwanted habits and the personality that had attached itself to me.

What I didn't understand was that Frank was teaching me that martial arts should be applied to everyday trials and tribulations. The spiritual and metaphysical aspects of the art will give us a competitive edge on the competition in the world. For example, if you engage in an argument or verbal battle with another party, you should utilize the same strategic approach from a martial arts perspective you would use in a physical battle, thinking out your moves with heavy consideration on how your opponent will react.

For the most part, I was unaware of how I was truly going to pull out of this depression. Until now. The tools were right there in front of me. I just had to learn how to use them effectively.

Not only was he coaching me how to become a better fighter, he was coaching me through life. He explained that I had a ton of negativity going on in my life, enough to cripple some of the toughest men. Frank told me I had to find a way to channel those negative emotions and turn them into positive energy. And when I was able to identify and utilize that strategy effectively, I would achieve greatness as a result of the conversion of energies.

"No question, Joe, you will be fighting an uphill battle for many days to come, but when you execute your goal, you will change your life into something great." He went on to tell me the difference between an executor and the guy who has a plan, a potential idea, or invention is that an executor sticks to a strict discipline and follows through, no matter how hard the struggles get. "If you become an executor, you will pull through this and become hardened and much stronger."

I now knew my training sessions were not just barbaric fighting sessions, as some people may have viewed them. They were therapeutic and had tremendous purpose for me. I was conditioning myself physically as well as mentally, preparing for any life challenge that lay ahead or within me.

He methodically conditioned me for the black belt grading that was only days away. Through the past months, we refreshed all the material I was previously graded on through my six-hour test. We fought, wrestled, grappled, and conditioned our bodies and minds for this test.

It was scheduled for August 5, 2004. Just my luck it was 97 degrees and humid out. I was ripped to shreds and cardio-conditioned into the best shape I had ever been in.

I arrived at his house at noon. Frank didn't want to grade me at 5:00 AM for several reasons. First, he wanted the heat to try and throw off my game. Second, he invited six other black belts to witness and participate in the event; they might not have shown at 5 AM. He was trying to physically and mentally wear me down. The mental fight started the minute the scenario changed; I walked into an unexpected situation.

He lined up the class in the ranks. He made sure the group was properly stretched out and was about to begin the grading when he asked, "Joe, are you ready? Teach the class, and demonstrate all the material. I know you perfected the material. You clearly exhibited it to me over the last weeks. To pass the test, you must effectively instruct the class on each and every piece of grading material for the next few hours. Then you have to fight all the black belts and then me. Ready, begin."

He threw me for a loop. The whole game changed, as had my life on the eleventh. He knew he was testing my executor abilities. I had to overcome this challenge right there and then to move on to engage my demons mentally over the next months.

After about four and a half hours of painstakingly instructing the critical audience in front of me, it was time to fight. I was worn down by the blazing sun and the emotionally strenuous last few hours, but I knew I had to follow through with this test. I wasn't just testing my abilities to teach the art or fight under extreme conditions. I was testing my willingness to execute a tough challenge before me. That day, those painful hours were serving as a cleansing of my soul. I was removing a piece of this unwanted life right there, and I had the support of the brotherhood of black belts I had grown close to over the last decade.

There were six experienced fighters I had to make it past, then to Master Barone. With the heat dominating my conditioned body, I knew I had to rely on my mind to get through the next hour. My drive, determination, and the character that was developed on these very grounds over the last few months would have to lead me to victory. I wasn't just facing these natural-born killers; I was facing the demons that had implanted themselves in my soul since the eleventh. It was time to roll. I was ready to do this.

As everyone circled around, I envisioned the people of the neighboring homes looking out their windows in awe, thinking that the ritual unfolding in their clear view resembled a movie where thugs surround a good guy.

With every fighter I moved past, Barone moved the circle in closer. When that took place, it was like the weapons of my fighting arsenal were getting taken away from me. I was fighting each fighter in gradual phases of skill. I fought first-degree, then second-degree, and then third-degree black belts. I was climbing the ladder to greatness that hot, humid August day. It replicated the Bruce Lee movie where he fought tougher opponents as he ran up the stairs to higher levels of fighters, until he reached the toughest, the master.

By the time I reached the fourth-degree black belt, Jay O'Keefe, I could barely stand. I was wounded prey in the presence of a ravenous predator. With a voracious look in his eyes, he was prepared to advance toward me with great force. Then I heard the voice of my mentor, "Joe, stick to game. If you don't make it through him and me, you have to do this all over again. Dig deep into your soul, search for whatever tools you need to get past him, and then I will be waiting for you. Don't give up. We all believe in you." I used that thirty seconds of inspiration to control my respiration and emotions and focus on the task at hand.

When Frank said, "Begin," the circle of fighters closed in on me. I was now fighting in a five-foot circle. With no room for error, I fought just to protect myself, fighting to keep my guard hands up. I wasn't even thinking of fighting offensively but just defending myself to survive this contest. I found myself weathering a tremendous storm of kicks and punches. I looked to Michael for strength and support to move past this. I became numb to the physical pain; I blasted out a barrage of accurate and forceful punches and had the fourth-degree, who outweighed me by at least fifty pounds, retreating back into those who were holding the circle. I clearly didn't defeat him, but I exhibited what Frank wanted me to do. I didn't give up. I was relentless in pursuing my goal.

I took a knee after Frank momentarily stopped the fight. He ordered me to stand. He looked me in the eye and told me, "We can end this right now, but you won't be validated. Or you can suck it up and follow through with something that will put you on a path to follow through with anything you set out to do in life. It is your choice." I knew this was a life-changing moment for me. Do I follow through with hopes of overcoming the depression that had been holding me down for the past three years, or do I surrender and succumb to every demon that has dominated me?

The six members who cleansed my soul through the battles that had just taken place were now cheering for me. They had never been fighting me; they had been battling the negativity that had been controlling me. Every punch or kick they landed weakened the substance of the negativity attached to me. They had been assisting me in the process I was going through.

Frank ordered the circle to open up and instructed Jay, the fourth-degree, to take control of the match. We lined up about three feet from each other, saluted Jay, then each other. I put my hands up, forcing them with all my might to protect my vital areas. I had to put my anxiety and exhaustion out of the equation. "Ready, begin." I was now at the mercy of Frank and Jay. Within seconds, I was on my back fighting to get back to my feet. This symbolized what the past three years had been like. This was my chance; it was now or never. I had to do this once and for all.

Exhausted as if an exorcism had been taking place within my body—actually, in a sense one had—I tried to extract any negativity within my body that had housed itself there as a result of the eleventh. I searched for a way to escape the strategically challenging position Frank had put me in. He began to rain down punishing strikes. At this point I couldn't see; I was blinded by either sweat or blood pouring into my eyes. I didn't have my eyesight; I had to rely on my other senses to get through. Despite my severely impaired sight, I was still trying to create an opening to escape before he put me in a submission hold.

I was praying to make it through. I was grappling with the idea of tapping out, a slang term for submitting to the challenge at hand, when an intense voice, that of a savior, screamed, "Break!" Sensei Jay, who was controlling the match, stopped the fight. I thought I caught a break, enough to rest and wipe my eyes dry to gain the most important sense necessary to fight back, my eyesight. He stood us up on the line and ordered the circle in tighter. At this point, I called out to the circle for a towel. Frank said, "Absolutely not. He doesn't get a break to wipe his face off. If you were on the street, you wouldn't ask your attacker for a towel if he split you open. Besides, your eyes can deceive you; use body relation to get through this." In that instant, I had come to the realization that what I saw that September morning with my own eyes had been controlling me. I had believed I could never recover from this depression. It was time to defeat this demon.

The fight concluded. It wasn't a matter of who was tougher that day, but if the tools I was given, as well as the instruction on how to use them, would guide me to overcome the challenges of the past, present, and future.

That scorching, agonizing August afternoon fulfilled my desire to establish the new beginning of my life. It was all the result of having the courage to call an old friend I had fallen out of touch a few years earlier. I would never have been able to become focused without his help. I learned how to execute goals once again. My newly found invigoration, and the tools I was given to become an executor, will help me make a difference in my life and the lives of many.

The Executor
Master Frank Barone, my inspirational instructor

Chapter 16

Calendar of Commitment

Back in the day, Mike and I, while aspiring to be firefighters, also dreamed of working hard and gaining one of twelve slots in the NYC Firefighters Calendar of Heroes.

There was no question: he had a competitive edge on me. Not only did he get on the job when I was still a police officer, he was in better shape than I. I was bigger, he was lean, and that's what the judges for the calendar looked for. At first, I didn't really focus much on it, because I knew the probability of doing it was slim. When he brought it up to me on several occasions, I told him although it sounded great, I wouldn't get in; he would. He committed to me that if I ever got on the job, we would set the goal and go at it together, side by side.

It wasn't until he was killed at the World Trade Center, and after Maria and I broke off our marriage, that I became committed to carrying out the goal of making it into the calendar, something Mike and I were supposed to do together.

I knew there were the tryouts for the calendar in February 2004. It was now the end of the summer, and to be honest, I knew if I tried out tomorrow, I would have no shot. As a matter of fact, the judges would probably tell me to not even take my shirt off and to forget the whole process.

But I knew I had about four months to train. Sixteen short weeks to work like a dog, as well as eat the healthiest foods this earth could produce. I now weighed 205 pounds; I had to shed at least twenty to be competitive.

I kept my goal to myself. I didn't want any of my firefighter brothers to catch wind of what I was doing, because they would bust my chops and taunt me every time they saw me. Besides, if my attempt failed, they would never let me live it down.

The training started off light but within two weeks was rapidly getting more and more demanding. I ran two miles a day for the first week, then three a day by the third week, and five miles by the one-month mark. At that point, I was running thirty-five miles a week. I had to use Sunday as a rest day. As I started the fifth week, I had already dropped about nineteen pounds. Now it was time to supplement with weights.

I added forty-five minutes a day of an accelerated weight-lifting program, which implemented twelve to fifteen repetitions with concentration on two body parts a day, plus the hard work of running six to eight miles a day.

My workouts lasted about two hours, but it wasn't enough. By the three-month mark, my progress, although great, was not enough to even be considered for the twelve slots.

The competition was intense. The job has twelve thousand members in it. Typically, about 10 percent show up over the course of a week to audition for the calendar. If I was even going to be considered, I had to push the bar even further.

One advantage I had over most was an immeasurable inspiration, a hero, my brother, someone who was supposed to be here doing this with me. I now had the job of doing it for both of us. The pressure just topped the scale at enormous.

It was now down to the wire. One week stood between me and the tryout. I was working the night tour at the firehouse, training in the firehouse gym with no shirt on. Even though it was winter, for some strange reason the gym was stifling hot. One of the brothers walked in, saw me with no shirt on, saw the progress, and knew right away what I was training for. As I lifted my dumbbells, a voice called out, "You're training for the calendar, aren't you, pretty boy? The cat is out of the bag now." I didn't want to lie, so I just laughed and told him we would all just have to wait and see.

I knew the next time I worked in the firehouse, every single member would be waiting to see me just to tease me. But I didn't care. Believe it or not, I wasn't doing this for me; after all, I was torturing myself emotionally and physically. I looked at it as another opportunity to make Mike's spirit live on, something he clearly requested in the letter he left us. I was doing this in the hopes of completing my goal, so the real story that would be told after it was done was that I did it because he inspired me, and because I knew it was something we wanted to do together. I wanted to keep my promise to him.

It was now the night before the tryouts. I reflected on the challenges I overcame. I started running two miles a day, passed eight, then ten, and pushed myself to almost break a long distance run of more than twenty miles a day. I dropped down to just about 6 percent body fat, almost a 20 percent drop from the first day of the fire academy.

I set my alarm to rise in the morning at 0600 hours. I weighed in that morning at exactly 177.5 pounds. I had dropped about thirty pounds, but one thing I couldn't drop was the anxiety that was building.

As I walked toward the auditorium in Metro Tech Center (Fire Headquarters), I was shocked to see the turnout for the tryout. The numbers were staggering. There were hundreds of competitors occupying the seats, crammed into the standing room, and lined double file down the halls and out the doors. The first thought that ran through my head was to turn around and go home. Someone who makes it into the calendar falls within the top .10 percent of the job. That's 1/10th of 1 percent.

I stood in line outside the building for about an hour and then moved into the lobby for about thirty minutes. By the time I got a seat in the auditorium and was assigned a number, I was starving. It was well past lunch; as a matter of fact, we were approaching dinner. As more and more time passed, I noticed several people getting out of their seats in total frustration and disgust and storming out of the auditorium, giving up on their goal of auditioning to make the calendar.

I must admit, I flirted with the idea of just getting up and leaving, but a voice in my head told me to stay and reminded me I had the support of the most inspirational person who touched my life, someone I knew who wanted to take this journey with me, side by side. So the notion of leaving was not an option.

It was almost dinnertime when they called my number. Though mentally and physically exhausted, I knew the show had to go on. I had to execute what I went there to do: make it into the calendar.

Famished but still driven, I walked into the room where the judges were conducting their duties. At that point, I wasn't even nervous; I had shaken that within the first three hours there. They asked me to take off my shirt, grab two firefighter tools—first an axe and then a six-foot hook—and give them the best pose possible.

When I was done, I put on my shirt and looked toward the panel of judges, male and female, and one of the female judges winked at me. I didn't believe it was a wink out of flirtation but a wink of acknowledgment, as well as what I believed to be a hint that I was what they were looking for. As I thanked them, they told me they would be in touch over the next thirty days, after the panel made its decision.

Although enormous, the suspense over the next thirty days really wasn't killing me. I knew I had an angel pulling for me, and whether I made it in, I had made drastic changes to my lifestyle, something that would live with me forever. And most of all, I kept my commitment to honor Mike's request of making his spirit live on.

One stormy afternoon, during a torrential rainstorm, I ran out to get the mail. The rain was coming down so hard that by the time I reached the mailbox, I barely could see in front of me. As I ran toward the front door of my home to retreat from the extreme element, I didn't realize the mail was getting soaked. By the time I set it on the countertop, took off my shoes, and picked up the mail, some pieces had become illegible due to their saturation with water.

What I did notice was a letter from Metro Tech with the fire department seal on the outside of the letter; I knew this letter had priority. I opened it, and as I did so, I noticed it was actually disintegrating in my hands. The only thing I could read at the top of the letter was, "Dear Joseph, We are pleased to," and then the rest was smudged. I did notice on the bottom that it contained contact information for a gentleman by the name of Alan Batt.

I reached out to Mr. Batt, and he explained that he was a photographer from the fire department who was in charge of shooting the calendar. I told him my name, and he said, "Joseph, congratulations. You are one of thirteen people I will be shooting for the 2005 Firefighters Calendar." At first I was taken aback, but then my wits kicked in. I did some quick math in my head, and asked Mr. Batt, "Why thirteen members?" I thought I still could be eliminated. Then he explained to me how the math worked: twelve inside, representing each month, and one on the cover.

The calendar came out in July of 2004. It hit the shelves in every major bookstore in the country as well as on the Internet. It also generated a lot of press because of my connection to Michael. The primary benefit to making the calendar was an opportunity to make his name live on. All of us donated our time at special events and on television shows, as well as calendar signings, educating the public about fire safety and fire prevention. It was very fulfilling to give back to the community; that is one of the benefits that comes with serving the public.

I could not have done this without the inspiration of my brother, Michael. His memory became an asset for me, helping me execute my dream of becoming a fraternal member of the calendar.

This was a period in my life when I made a definitive statement to become committed to a calendar of future events that would guarantee the longevity of making his memory live on.

Mike, although you were not here physically to share the experience, we still did it together.

Mr. January 2005
Me posing for the shot in Times Square, NYC

Chapter 17

Living for the Moment

By the fall of 2003, I had been dating several women but had no success in meeting the right person. I began to believe that the love life I was living would get no better. Romance seemed like it was not in my cards. I accepted the fact that I may have been put on this earth just to be alone.

I was on a weekend firehouse trip to Chicago to watch the Cubs play the Pirates. This proved to be an exciting event, because the Cubs needed every win in the race for the playoffs. I invited Jerome to come with us, and without hesitation, he packed his bags. With excitement in the air, I knew great times would be had this weekend.

These trips served as a release valve for the pressures and depression that surrounded me in New York. I think Jerome went out of his way to accompany me on many of these road trips because he wanted to support me. He didn't care what the reason for the trip was, he just cared for me and realized that when I was out of town and away from the bad memories of what had taken place back home, I was the old Joe for a brief moment, unscathed by the eleventh.

We were inseparable, like the dynamic duo; it seemed as if we never went anywhere alone. At this point in my life, I truly needed the full support of someone who was by my side when those buildings fell. It made it easier for me.

On the third day of our five-day trip, we had already watched the baseball game and gone out to the local bars and clubs; we had an unquenchable thirst for more excitement. Jerome came up with the idea of changing our flights and coming home two days early. At first I wrestled with the idea, because I knew I would be returning home to the recurring memories and horrific flashbacks, but I decided to roll the dice and take my chances and hope we wouldn't crap out. I agreed. The only thing we had to do was change our flights, and it would come at no small expense to someone.

Jerome was dating a girl, Nicole, at the time, nothing too serious, but I had a feeling she was not for him. She was employed by Continental Airlines at the time of our trip. He phoned her and asked if she could change our flight or provide buddy passes for us to get home. She said she would honor the request only if he was going to spend the night with her. He told her we had something to do when we landed; that's why we needed the early flight back.

She wasn't happy at all. She said she had the ability to fly both of us home; however, she didn't want to accommodate me because she felt as if I was taking him away from her that night. So she told him, "For you I will do it, but for Joey, no way." After about a fifteen-minute verbal phone brawl, he made his point, got his way, and had the tickets waiting for us at the airport at no cost to us. She would be the one who would pay the price.

We arrived at the gate, checked in, and were greeted by an obnoxious host we handed our tickets to. Nicole must have called the Continental Airlines gate and told this person to make it very rough for us before we boarded, because the man demanded we wear a collared shirt and tie, saying it was protocol for using a buddy pass. We were dressed in jeans and golf shirts. We tried to explain diplomatically to the employee of Continental Airlines that we would have no problem following his orders; we did have collared shirts, but they were wet, dirty, and severely wrinkled from the night before. He didn't seem to care. He told us that if we didn't follow his orders, the plane would surely leave without us.

We donned the wet, dirty, disgusting shirts and were on our way. After liftoff, we took them off and wore our golf shirts. We were now well on our way to continuing an already exciting weekend.

We landed and went directly to my apartment to take showers and freshen up before we embarked on our journey to Hoboken, New Jersey, a swanky upscale area that afforded us the fast-paced night we were looking for.

We ate at Frankie and Johnny's Steakhouse and then hit the strip. We walked into different bars but weren't satisfied with the atmosphere. So we decided to walk to the PATH train and take a five-minute ride into Manhattan.

On the train headed to the city, we couldn't help but reflect on the eleventh. We spoke about how we crossed the Hudson together on that September morning and how it changed our lives forever. He comforted me and told me not to worry. This time, the ride wouldn't be so significant that our lives would be drastically changed as we crossed the choppy waters. Little did we know he was wrong. This time, we were on a train that would, once again, write both of our destinies.

After about two hours in the city, it was approaching 1:00 AM, and I was very tired from the long weekend. I decided to let him know I had enough and wanted to leave. He agreed, and we made our way back to our hometown, which at the time was on Staten Island.

As Jerome drove home, he was bartering to try and make me come with him to our neighborhood hot spot, the Level One Lounge. It was about 2:00 AM, and I was exhausted. He dropped me off at home and went to the lounge by himself.

It wasn't until the next morning that he told me he had an amazing time at the lounge. He had met who he believed to be his next girlfriend. He told me I knew her. The name Jessica Whitmore at first didn't ring a bell. He went on to describe her and tell me all the details. I had never seen Jerome this way about a female. He usually dated several women to see who was right for him, but this time, something gave me the feeling he was serious about what he was saying. He told me from this point on, he would be exclusive with her.

After meeting her, I could see why he felt that way about her. She was beautiful. But let's put looks aside; she made every person in her company feel warm. I felt as if I had known her my entire life. She was a true homebody with one goal in mind: to treat my friend very well, and for that, she was okay in my book.

As the first few days went by, I was around them a lot. Obviously, Jerome was encouraging Jessica to set me up with one of her friends. At first, Jessica could not think of anyone who would be a perfect fit.

One day while I was with them in Manhattan, as they were searching for a Halloween costume to wear together to a party, Jessica told me she wanted to fix me up with her friend Stephanie. I asked her what her last name was. She told me Vernaci, and I immediately knew who she was. I had never met her, but I could put a name with the face, because my cousin Nicky went to school with her, and she used to date one of Nicky's friends, Frank Giordano, about ten years earlier. I remembered her to be beautiful and heard from Jessica she was a good person. Stephanie wasn't dating anyone at the time. We were both in a transitional period in our dating lives, so I said what the heck. It would be my first blind date.

After about a week and a half, I asked Jessica what was going on with Stephanie. Maybe she wasn't interested; I just wanted to see where I stood. Jessica told me that she had given her my number, and she didn't know why she hadn't called. She was persistent about wanting to call her to see what was going on, but I told her cockily, "Tell her she is beat. She had her chance and blew it."

That same night, I was at the Yankee vs. the Boston Red Sox game. It was the postseason, the second game of the ALCS. I had nothing else on my mind except the Yankees defeating their archrivals that night. All of a sudden, my phone rang; it was Jessica. She told me Stephanie said she was too shy to call. She told Jessica to give me her number and have me call her.

Go Yanks
Jerome Crimi, me, Frank Iervasi, Vinnie Varriano

From the left-field bleacher seats at Yankee Stadium, at the bottom of the third inning, I decided to call Stephanie to break the ice and knock out any awkwardness that may have existed. She could barely hear me, because as she said hello, a Yankee had simultaneously driven in a run to take the lead over the Red Sox. I told her who I was and asked her if she would like to go to dinner with me. She said sure but to call her after the game so she could hear me.

I was a bit nervous, I must admit. I was unsure if she was trying to blow me off or if she was serious about speaking later. After the game, believe it or not, I had come down with a violent case of food poisoning. The whole car ride home I was vomiting. It got so bad that another friend, Frank Iervasi, who had come to the game with us, was actually scared I might not make it through the night. He walked me into my apartment and stayed with me for quite some time and later called to check on me when he got home. Although I was extremely ill, I made an effort to call Stephanie. I dialed her number, and she picked up and said hello with an angelic tone. But as much as I wanted to talk with her, I told her I wasn't feeling well and would call her the next day from work. I had made a commitment to her that I would call her after the game, and I wanted to assure her although I attended a game, I had no intention of playing games with her.

I struggled to make it into work at my firehouse in midtown Manhattan the next morning. I was still violently ill. The men at the firehouse recognized how sick I was and suggested I take the detail that was going out to Ladder 35 that day. They told me to rest in the TV room until I felt better.

I lay down in a reclining chair underneath a blanket all day. I didn't seem to be getting any better. When the members of the fire company announced it was lunchtime, I didn't even get out of the chair. I was more worried about calling Stephanie that day than I was about feeling better.

We spoke on the phone several times over the next few days. I wanted to align myself to ask her on a date the coming Friday night. The plans were set. I felt about 85 percent better. I headed to pick her up about 7:00 PM. I had made reservations at a phenomenal steakhouse in Fair Lawn, New Jersey, the River Palm Terrace.

I called her about five minutes to seven, as I turned onto her block, to let her know I was going to be there in two minutes. Traditionally I would go to the door to pick up my date and introduce myself to the family. However, I had recently experienced mixed emotions about that from my recent dates: some wanted me to meet their family, but some thought I was ballsy showing up at the front door, because it was too early for me to meet their family. So I put the ball in her court. If she said, "Come in a minute," I would have had no problem going in. But she said, "I will be right out." As I pulled up to the house, she was already walking out to my truck.

She opened the door and climbed into my truck. I was in awe; she was beautiful. She had an exotic look about her, and those beautiful, dark brown eyes took my breath away. We both said hello and began our trip to New Jersey. The conversation flowed very nicely. I felt as if I had known her for years. Believe it or not, we got stuck in the worst traffic, and to top it off, I got lost. But at the end of the day, it didn't matter. The company was amazing, and I was in the presence of the most beautiful girl I had ever met.

Finally, an hour and a half later, we arrived at the restaurant. We broke bread for the first time. For some, the thought of being on a blind date and having dinner with the person might have been awkward, but for us it seemed as natural as breathing.

We went out for drinks in Manhattan after dinner. The wine was flowing as well as the conversation. I remember looking into her eyes and thinking this might actually be the one. As crazy as that might sound, it was my gut telling me this.

I dropped her off just after one o'clock. I leaned over and gave her a kiss on the cheek and said, "I hope we can do this again." At that point, she asked if I wanted to go to her nieces, Jade and Gabrielle's, soccer game the next day at Miller Field in Staten Island. I absolutely seized the opportunity to be in her presence again.

The next morning, I picked her up about 10:00 AM. We headed over to the field, parked the car, got out, and walked toward the activity on the field. As I approached what I believed was a large group of parents and family rooting for their children, I was shocked to see this crowd all look toward our direction and warmly greet Stephanie. For a quick second I thought she might have withheld the fact that she was the team leader or coach or something of that magnitude. But I was wrong; it was her entire family. Brothers, cousins, sisters, aunts, uncles, parents, friends, neighbors, and so on and so on! I guess she got me back for not ringing her doorbell fifteen hours earlier.

If this wasn't awkward, I don't know what is. Luckily, I am as social as they come. I am not shy, nor did I mind the presence of her entire family tree. I was welcomed with open arms by a family that is as close knit as they come. My status with Stephanie was elevated from not just being another guy.

I wasn't the only one feeling positive vibes in the air. Stephanie, as time went on, revealed to me that on that soccer field, the day after our first date, she told her friend Megan that she thought I was going to turn out to be the one. Little did we know that our vibes would become a serious reality. We were inseparable right from the start. The process of falling in love with her came easily, naturally, and without hesitation. As time went on, we knew the commitment we had to each other would not be broken.

As we approached our one-year anniversary, I remember Stephanie sitting me down and telling me the fast-paced life I was living, although productive, would eventually take its toll on me. She went on to tell me I needed to stop and live for the moment and that I should savor life as it was unfolding right in front of me. "You can never get time back," she went on to tell me. "You owe it to yourself to live for the moment you are a part of."

This was a request from her I had a hard time honoring. As much as it made sense, I felt that Michael's life was stolen from him at such a young age, and by witnessing this, I tried to do as much as possible as fast as I could in my life. I feared my life could be cut just as short as his.

I grappled with the thought of living a free, slow-paced life. I knew that was what Steph wanted for me, for us. It was imperative for me to start savoring the moments alongside her if I wanted to solidify longevity in the relationship.

"Stephanie, I love you with all my heart. You are my soul mate, and for us, I will do whatever it takes to lead a life that follows your advice to live for the moment."

Soul Mate
Stephanie and me on a dinner date

Chapter 18

Rebirth of Happiness

As the days turned into weeks and then months and years, my mother's character and personality seemed to be in the same slumber she had walked the earth with since the morning her life changed forever. After a mother loses her child, her baby, she can never be the same again; there will forever be a vacancy in her heart.

My mother had been searching for many years for a remedy for her pain of losing Michael. We all were. Nothing seemed to ease her pain until she received a phone call from my sister, Kim, in the early part of 2004, telling her she was pregnant. We all felt amazing excitement, anticipating the arrival of the new addition to the family.

As months went by and Kim got close to her due date, my mother was very busy staging a nursery in her house to get ready to babysit the little one. Stephanie and I were putting the finishing touches on our engagement party, which was scheduled for Sunday, November 21, 2004.

I was ecstatic that month because of the confirmation of my engagement to Stephanie as well as the imminent arrival of the baby. Little did I know these two great things in my life would happen with a bang.

The Sunday morning of our party, we were rushing around, trying to tie up all the loose ends before our entire families would meet, some for the first time. As the guests were starting to flow into the party about 5:00 PM, I received a cell phone call from Kim, informing me that she was going into labor.

We had changed the date of our party several times to accommodate my cousins, who had other engagements to attend on the previous dates. As a result of moving the party, several complications arose. It would become problematic for all my family to attend, as there was another family party scheduled for the same day. This put my family in a position of having to choose between my engagement party to Steph or another family party in Long Island. Miscommunication between the families resulted in a small number of my family members attending my event. Plus my sister wouldn't be able to make it. To add further insult to injury, my cousin, someone I looked up to my entire life, the man who was stepping into Michael's role that special day, my best man, chose not to attend my engagement party but to go to our other cousin's wedding. I understood and was okay with the fact that most of my family would attend the wedding. After all, they would come to my wedding the next year. However, my cousin should have known the significance behind the role he was stepping into that day. Michael was never recovered, and I looked to my cousin to fill in the role of being my best man. He wouldn't show, and that hurt me tremendously. We both decided it would be better if he stepped down as best man.

For the wedding, I asked someone who had the same family values as I did, someone who knew and cared about Michael, someone who recognized the deep importance of stepping into the role of a hero, Gennaro Manza.

Best Man
Gennaro and my mother, Linda

The next day around 7:00 PM, the Monday after our party, was when the real celebration would begin. There she was, Christina Michael Prince. Her middle name was in remembrance of a hero she would never meet. With the birth of this amazing cherub came a rediscovered ray of light on my mother's face.

As the months went by, it seemed to be getting easier for my mother to cope with the eleventh. Her daily visits to see her first grandchild gave her something to look forward to, a retreat from the disaster, and she loved every minute of it.

In May 2006, almost a year after we married, Stephanie became pregnant. When we told my family the news, my mother felt an unfamiliar heightened level of joy and excitement. It felt amazing to see happiness radiate from her face once again. The feeling of everyone in our family at witnessing a partial recovery in her spirit was immeasurable.

My daughter was born on January 26, 2007. Named Francesca Lynn, after her grandmother Fran and Nana Linda, she brought an instantaneous joy to everyone's lives. My mother was also showing great progress and focus in her life once again. All the pieces started to fall back together.

As I witnessed the birth of Francesca, I was also witnessing the rebirth of happiness within my family. What amazed us all about her was how much she looked like her Uncle Mikey and Nana Linda. We all felt like our family was moving in a positive direction. My sister and I had brought new lives to the family, and as a result, some of the void in my mother's heart was being filled.

I cried the moment Francesca was born. She was beautiful, crying at the top of her lungs. It wasn't until then I concretely realized that Michael wouldn't be there to high-five me and probably light up a cigar right there in the labor and delivery section.

Rebirth of Happiness
My father and mother holding Francesca Lynn

I held my daughter's hand for the first time as the doctor cut off the remnants of the umbilical cord. The unity from that point on has been as strong as steel. I was once again feeling a rare but tremendous amount of joy in my heart.

I have always heard of what the father-daughter bond was like from various people. Sayings like, "Daddy's little girl," or "Daddy's little princess" exemplified what some may have thought about their relationships with their daughters. But for me, it was that plus much more. My whole entire life changed the day she was born. I looked in her eyes for the first time and told her I would always be there for her. I made a commitment to her that I would forever be right by her side forever.

I know that if Michael were here with us, he would have been an amazing uncle to her, someone who would have embraced her with all his love and care. We would never have the opportunity to witness it, but I am positive that as he is looking down at her, he is smiling as much as we are. She will forever be a piece of him, and he will live on through her forever, through all the stories we reflect on in her presence.

She was everything I needed in my life to put me on a clear path to happiness again. I had the privilege of being married to one of the greatest women who has ever walked this earth, as well as my little baby girl, who truly brought back the happiness for all of us whose souls were buried deep beneath the rubble at Ground Zero.

To Lady Francesca and any future children I become blessed with, I will forever strive to be a role model in your life. I vow to love you to eternity, to be a daddy and a best friend, and I will teach you the values necessary to be caring people. You are forever in my heart.

Best friends
Daddy and Francesca

Family
Daddy, Francesca, and Mommy

Christina Michael my niece.
Named after her Uncle Mike.

Chapter 19

Rebuilding a Foundation

It was evident that the foundation of our family had collapsed in a fashion similar to the buildings on that beautiful fall morning in 2001. As America vowed to rebuild the foundations of those buildings, I vowed to rebuild our family and simultaneously bring back Michael. We needed to put every single piece of our lives back together, one brick at a time.

If we couldn't experience Michael's greatness in the physical life, he would live on through others who exhibited similar characteristics. We would award other people's achievements that mirrored many aspects of Michael's short time on this earth.

We set out to build the F. F. Michael Cammarata Foundation. The original visionary was my mother, Linda. With the hard work and help of Maria, we were able to form a nonprofit organization named the Firefighter Michael Cammarata Foundation. With the birth of this organization came an occupation that would help my mother cope with the loss of her son.

I became chairman of the board and participated in all decision-making about how we were going to allocate the funds in a fashion that would help Michael's spirit live on.

The organization gave scholarships to students at the Tottenville High School who were standout athletes and needed financial assistance to continue their studies and go on to college.

Proceeds were accumulated through various events that we organized. The first event we hosted was the first annual Firefighter Michael Cammarata charity hockey game. I strategically assembled a team of all the players Mike and I played with over the years. They would unite and form a team to play the actual NYC Firefighters ice hockey team. This was a team that had its eye on Mike the moment he was sworn in. As a matter of fact, on the morning of the eleventh, at 1100 hours, he was supposed to be attending a tryout in Suffolk County, Long Island, for the Firefighters hockey team. But because he was a probie, new in the firehouse, he did not want to ask for the time off or for a mutual tour exchange with another member. If he had gone, he would be here with us now.

After a ton of organization by my mother, Maria, and Jennifer, as well as all the members from Ladder 11, the game was a great success. Although the team that I formed, the Faces, named after my brother, lost 4–2, what all of us who participated in that event took away from the arena that day was empowering and extraordinary.

There is no greater reward to one's soul than volunteering your time for a good cause, having the event turn out to be a success, and then using the generous donations from everyone to impact positively the lives of the ones who are granted opportunities by the foundation. This is exactly what Michael's life was all about: positively impacting the lives of everyone he touched in the short time he was here.

As time went on, I crossed paths with an old friend of Mike's and mine who also played the great sport of hockey with us. This was our longtime friend and net minder, an individual who always gave 100 percent to whatever he did, someone who always fought for what he believed in: Joseph R. Cartigiano.

He came to my family and told us he had been the head coach of a youth program at the local ice arena. He wanted to organize a large hockey tournament in memory of Michael. He had a vision of making the invitational tournament so large that teams in the NHL would hear about it. And boy, was he right. He was able to gain the support of the New York Islanders. Their generosity of signed memorabilia and jerseys, as well as handwritten letters from the high-ranking managerial members of the organization, all contributed to the day's success.

Joe Cartigiano's hard work, as well as the hard work of everyone else, brought a tremendous joy to my mother's face. She was full of gratitude for what Joe had done for us. He truly is an amazing person.

The proceeds from that event provided full hockey equipment and seasonal dues to children of financially challenged families who wanted to play or continue to play the sport.

Sponsorships in Mike's honor lived on through many children and young adults from Little League Baseball to competitive high school scholarships in various different areas. The work of the Firefighter Michael Cammarata Foundation brought solace to the lives of my family, especially my mother. She always associates the recipients with Michael, pointing out how a particular characteristic about them reminds her of Michael.

The organization was one of the first building blocks that would contribute to rebuilding the foundation of our family. Its day-to-day operation and the objectives it sets out to do will forever preserve what Michael lived and died for.

Presentation of Michael's Jersey
L→R My mother, Linda, father, Joseph, Nanny Josephine,
Joseph Cartigiano, Stephanie, and me.

Chapter 20

America's Mayor

It is quite clear that when a tragedy occurs, whether it be what happened on the eleventh, a hurricane such as Katrina, or a tsunami like the one that hit Indonesia in 2004, millions of lives are impacted, and not just the lives that were directly affected. Nations, societies, and individuals band together, boys turn into men, heroes are made, and we look to our leaders for strength and resolve.

The leader who was clearly by my family's side as well as the nation's after the eleventh was Rudy Giuliani. He was nicknamed America's mayor after the eleventh because he united the country as a whole by exhibiting his ability to lead in the face of chaos. His genuine sincerity shined a bright light on every New Yorker during a great time of darkness, especially in my life.

I recently reflected on the time my entire family was at Michael's Fire Academy graduation, where we posthumously accepted his diploma. Rudy shook hands with me, looked me in the eyes with tremendous sincerity, and told me if I ever needed anything he would be there for me. It wasn't until the earlier part of 2009 that I would reach out to him with hopes of receiving a personal letter from him recommending me for law school. Within weeks of my request, I received a phone call from Ms. Hatton, the assistant to Mr. Giuliani. I was invited to his office to speak with him about my request.

Nervous about meeting with him, this time with a request, my friend Ronn Pearson left me with a piece of advice, "Joe, don't be nervous. Rudy is a human being; he puts his pants on one leg at a time just like you and me. I am sure you know he is sincere and caring. He is an expert at making people feel comfortable. Don't sweat it."

It was late January 2009. I was heading to Manhattan to meet with a world icon, a hero to millions of people. I was extremely nervous about being late, so I arrived two hours early. This was probably the worst thing I could have done, because the anticipation of meeting him again, along with the enormous request I was about to ask of him, was giving me ants in my pants. I couldn't sit still.

He wanted to see me 10:30 AM. I signed in at the front desk in the main lobby and waited for security to call up to see if I was authorized to go up to his office. I was granted a visitor's pass and was told to go directly to the elevator and push a certain number.

As the elevator began to rise, so did my blood pressure. Usually I am not a nervous person, but it is not every day that you meet with a person of this caliber, someone who was a top contender in the race for the White House just a few months earlier.

I got off the elevator and it seemed as though I couldn't feel my legs. There was only one other time in my life that I go off an elevator and had that similar feeling. I was visiting the Stratosphere in Las Vegas in 1998 and took the elevator to the roof. I stepped off and lost my bearings. The only difference was I was more than a thousand feet up at the time, so I couldn't understand why it was happening again.

I was greeted by a secretary. I told her who I was, and she made a call. Afterward, she said, "Someone will be right out to get you." I sat in the beautiful waiting area for only a few moments. I heard footsteps echoing from a long hallway. At that point, I looked at my watch; it was exactly 10:30 am.

The footsteps intensified as they got closer. A woman walked over to me and introduced herself as Beth. She said, "The mayor is waiting for you. Right this way."

We walked down a long hallway that resembled a gallery with the sole purpose of preserving photos and artifacts from September 11. I could clearly see Mr. Giuliani in several of the photos from Ground Zero. We walked a little further and turned a corner. Ms. Hatton told me the letter I wrote Mr. Giuliani was powerful and beautiful. I thanked her, as I walked by the United States of America flag, the City of New York flag, and the Office of the

Mayor of the City of New York flag, all exhibited in the well-lit hallway right before his office. As we made one more turn, I walked past two more assistants.

Then a door opened from the inside, and there he was: Rudy Giuliani. With great poise, he said, "Good morning, Joseph, it is great to see you again. Welcome, have a seat." One thing I'd thought might be intimidating was if I had to sit across a desk or table from him. But that wasn't the case. He pulled out a seat for me, and we sat a few feet from each other. There was no desk to serve as a barrier between us. Ronnie was right; he was an expert at making me feel comfortable in his presence.

We spoke about my goal and dream of going to law school. He gave me some of the most amazing advice about life and what to expect from life once I obtained a law degree. He also asked about my family and how we were doing since the eleventh. I saw an amazing amount of concern and sincerity expressed. I told him about my mother's debilitating disease that was getting the better of her, and he gave me advice on how to stay strong and how I should look to the ones closest in my life for support.

We spent just about an hour together; it was one of the most amazing moments of my life. He validated everything I ever thought he was and gave me the letter recommending me for law school. He showed me, and the world, he truly is a man of his word.

In my eyes, he picked up those buildings, the city, and the country and walked us into a positive direction. And for that, he is a true hero to me and the entire world.

Presentation of GOP Painting.
L→R Ken Rosenbaum, me, Rudy Giuliani, and Mary Sansone, the founder of C.I.A.O

Chapter 21

Demise of a Matriarch

Looking back, two years before the events of September 11, 2001, we were blessed with the news that my mother had beaten breast cancer. After extensive surgery and a long journey of chemotherapy, which physically incapacitated her, she fought an uphill battle with one thing in mind: to survive for the betterment of her family. We all were given a second chance at life and the privilege of living on as a happy, healthy family. None of us knew what the next two years were about to unleash on us.

From that point on, with the new lease on our family, not one of us took life for granted. We enjoyed every possible moment. We grew stronger as a family. It wasn't just my mother battling the disease; we all were fighting it and shared the triumph of victory together.

As our mother, Linda, watched the towers crumble to the ground, sitting in our kitchen and watching TV, she was diagnosed with a terminal destiny. In my eyes, every time I saw her after that day, her life expectancy was being rapidly reduced. From that second on, she would never be the same person she was before.

She must have organized an emotional manhunt trying to bring Michael home. Knowing she couldn't physically go down to Ground Zero to search for him added an enormous amount of anxiety. He was missing, but she knew where her baby was. It was just a matter of waiting and hoping, and that, in itself, was eating at her very soul. As the days passed and we heard no news, you would see the pain in her eyes. I know she had the feeling of impending doom, it was written on her face, and we all felt the same pain. But a mother, who at this time could not account for her young, would house the most pain of anyone in the family.

Two weeks after the disaster, I couldn't bear to look her in the eye. Suffering from survivor's guilt, I thought when she looked at me she would associate the life I was living with the death of Michael. I guess that it was natural for her to think like that. Mike and I were very close; side by side, we experienced the best things life had to offer.

It became quite evident, as more time was going by, that emotional rigor mortis was setting into my mother's mind. She had to deal with the difficult truth that Michael was never coming home alive, and it ate away at her, piece by piece. I began to take on a second source of pain as a result: first losing my brother, and second, watching my mother suffer emotionally. This was worse than anything I had to experience in my entire life.

She began to smoke again, despite doctor's orders. She tried to explain to us that it took the edge off and had nothing to do with her previous addiction to nicotine. Whatever the reason, she had given it up right after her diagnosis with breast cancer and had been a nonsmoker for two years. Now it seemed like she was desperately trying to make up for lost time.

I was very worried about her; we all were. I tried to be the voice of reason in her life. I tried to counsel her to give up smoking. I explained to her she needed to do something else to cope with the demons of the eleventh besides ensuring a slow, painful death that cigarettes were capable of orchestrating. She answered by telling me she would stop soon and that she went for regular doctor follow-ups since the cancer. I knew she was trying to pacify me, but I didn't want to pressure her too much, too fast. I wanted her to quit, not smoke even more. I knew I had to back off.

As time went on, I believed my mother would never be the same spiritually. Part of her had been stolen, gone forever. She knew she would never be with her youngest son again. Living with that, the pain seemed to have gotten worse for her. To ease her pain, she and my father started to travel to their vacation condo in Florida.

Florida was a place she could be her old self for a while. She would constantly speak about her next trip to the condo. It served as an emotional retreat from her days of suffering back in the city.

It was a good three years after the eleventh before I saw signs of recovery from within my mother's soul. With the birth of her first grandchild, Christina Michael Prince, a beautiful baby girl, would come a newly discovered vigor.

Finally, there was fresh life in our family, as well as on my mother's face. I hoped that this would be the turning point for my mother's mental recovery.

The eventual unity of Stephanie and me in marriage in 2005 also added happiness in my mother's life. She helped plan the wedding day. After all, she had grown very close to Stephanie; she eventually would love her like a daughter. As a matter of fact, she told me numerous times how she felt about Steph and refreshed my mind, telling me how lucky I was to have someone so special in my life.

Stephanie became pregnant in May 2006. Through her pregnancy, we all started to see a change for the better in my mother's emotional battle with the eleventh. It seemed like she finally had something amazing to look forward to again in her life. My daughter, Francesca Lynn, was born on January 26, 2007. She brought an instantaneous joy to everyone's lives.

My mother was still smoking heavily, and I would constantly try to get my point across to her about quitting. I offered to take her to the doctor so they could prescribe the patch. She tried it but claimed to have had a reaction. I tried to get her to try other types of aids, such as different nicotine chewing gums. She seemed to be resistant to my methods. Quitting cold turkey would have never been an option for her; when those towers fell, it buried any will that she had left.

In July 2007, my mother, one of the greatest people in the world, planned my thirtieth surprise party for me. She did an amazing job in organizing and executing the party. The only thing was, I saw the excitement on her face the week before the party and knew exactly what she had planned. Although I may not have been surprised, I greatly appreciated her efforts. But most of all, I knew she had the time of her life planning it. That was the best gift to me: to see her have the will and motivation to carry out the plans for such a big event all by herself. That was what really brought me happiness that day.

That July night, I danced with my beautiful, healthy, and vibrant mother for the last time.

Last Dance
My beautiful mother and I dancing for the last time

Little did we know she had a rapidly growing disease hidden deep in her body that would show its ugliness in the very near future.

She and my father began building their Florida dream house in August of 2007. She was excited to go through the entire process. Building a home may be very stressful to some, but to her, she knew she was building a new life, a fresh start in Florida, a place she said she and my father would retire and grow old together, side by side.

In early November 2007, as the building of their home was moving along, so was the progression of disease in her body. It was quite unexpected. She was going to have a small, routine procedure done at the doctor's, so she had to go for routine pre-op testing. There it was; it showed itself for the first time in a chest X-ray. It appeared to be only two centimeters, about the size of a medium-sized acorn, nestled in the upper lobe of her left lung.

We all hoped it wasn't serious. But when we were waiting for the results of the test to be confirmed, she told us that back in July, about the same time as my surprise party, she had gotten back her blood work. It came back with some issues, but she had ignored it. At that point, I knew it was cancer. I didn't need a doctor to tell me. The bad blood work, coupled with her aggressive smoking habits, was a recipe for disaster.

Two days later, the bad news and our worst nightmares were confirmed. Stricken with cancer the second time, this one unrelated to the breast cancer, she was diagnosed with stage 3 lung cancer. Again my mother was going to face a tremendous challenge. We as an entire family were going to face this challenge together.

I had great concerns this time around. Was she going to have the will to survive? It seemed like part of her had given up on life the eleventh, the day she lost her son. I was nervous she would refuse the treatments.

The surgery to remove the acorn-sized mass was scheduled immediately. It was now the Monday before Thanksgiving. She had been in surgery for about four and a half hours. I was terrified she wouldn't come out alive. This was a major procedure; all I hoped for was that she had survived the operation.

The surgeon, Dr. Piccone, a seventy-five-year-old man, had been a surgeon for over a half of century, came out of the operating room with a worn look on his face. He resembled a boxer who lasted fifteen rounds, fought with all his might, but lost by decision. He said, "Guys, I have very bad news."

The pit in my stomach dropped, and I became weak at the knees, dizzy, and almost incoherent. I anxiously awaited the crushing news that was going to come out of his mouth. "The tumor was five and a half centimeters, about the size of a handball. I did everything I could. I removed it, and she is in recovery. She did great, but I am worried about the size. If I would have know it was over four centimeters, I wouldn't have operated. But it was hidden, and I was very far in. Instead of sewing her back up, I took a chance and removed it." He went on to tell us he had to remove almost three-quarters of her lung. If it's true size had been known from the start, and it was inoperable, she would have been categorized as stage 4 lung cancer, which has a poor survival rate; after one year, only 30 percent survive.

When she woke from recovery, I looked her in the eye and thought she looked like she was dead. She resembled what my grandfather looked like when he died from smoking when I was ten years old, a sight that haunts me to this day. I was fighting back the tears. I didn't want her to see me like this. I didn't want her to think the odds were stacked against her like I knew they were. I wanted to fight right there alongside her. Part of me wished it was me who had the disease. I knew I would have the drive and the fight within me to beat it. I was unsure she had the will to go on in life; she wanted to be with Michael. I wish I could have taken the disease from her, sparing her life right then and there.

She immediately started chemotherapy, as well as radiation in the form of tomotherapy, an isolated form of targeted area radiation that offers a concentrated dose of radiation to a particular spot.

Three months into treatment, they gave her a full-body scan, searching for any re-growth within the lung or new growth within the body.

She seemed to be free from any new cancer except a pea-sized growth on her arm that would prove to be cancer. I immediately knew this was a bad sign. That it had appeared on her arm must have meant the cancer cells had journeyed throughout her body.

After six months, the radiation and chemo had taken their toll on my mother. She was weak and had to rest after her sessions. When she had time off from her treatments, you wouldn't even believe this woman had a common cold let alone an aggressive form of cancer that was dismantling her faculties day after day.

It was now June. She seemed to have been responding well to the treatment, until one day when she was in the mall with my father. She had ventured off to the ladies department in Macy's while my father went to the men's department. After about thirty minutes, he headed to the section of the store where he believed she was shopping. All of a sudden, he saw her walking around aimlessly, scared, in a trance, with her left arm extended straight out in front of her like a zombie. He ran to her aid. She was not cognizant of her surroundings or whereabouts. It took a good fifteen minutes for her to come to and regain control of her arm. Unaware of what had happened, they went home and she lay in bed.

When I got the phone call about what had just occurred, I encouraged them to go to the doctor. I left my home to meet them. She had experienced a small seizure and hadn't been able to control her arm. The doctor immediately ordered a brain scan.

Within two days, we got the grim news. The cancer had spread to her brain. Four spots, in two separate quadrants of her brain, were now controlling her faculties. I remember getting the news via cell phone, as I was driving down Route 18 in New Jersey. I hung up the phone and broke down into tears. I knew it was getting the better of her. I knew this wouldn't turn out well.

When I raced to her house, I knew I would have to encourage her to keep fighting. She knew she would have a tough battle ahead of her. She would now start an aggressive chemo, coupled with a chemo pill and brain radiation.

She endured this demanding treatment for several more weeks; we then awaited the next scan that was weeks away. The hardest thing was waiting those two days for the results. We all had the feeling it wouldn't be good, but we had to know the results.

It was now August. I knew she only had a few more months left. It wasn't about beating the cancer anymore but cheating it out of more time before it claimed her life. I was faced with a tremendous decision. I was now thirty-one. I had returned to college over the last year and a half to finish my bachelor's degree from St. John's University, something my mother always wanted me to complete. The problem was I had eighteen more credits left, six classes standing in the way of receiving my degree. I wanted her to be alive to see me finish my undergraduate studies. Do I take the six classes and the workload that comes with six days of school, plus a fifty-hour work week, and a fulltime marriage, and a father-daughter relationship while my mother is dying just to finish by December? Or do I split the six classes into two semesters and finish in May?

I knew I had a lot on my plate, but I wanted my mother to see me finish. So I did it. I positioned myself to take it all on at once and finish in December, because I feared she wouldn't make the new year.

I managed to work fifty hours a weeks, go to the university fulltime, be a husband and a dad, and actually see my mother every day on my way to school. I saw her more than I ever had before. I made it work, and to top it off, I made her proud; I finished my last semester with a 3.73 GPA and landed on the Dean's List.

We had organized a sixtieth surprise party for her. We invited all of her friends and family. She was surely going to be surprised. It was 8:00 PM the eve before the party when my father called me with the news that she had another seizure. This time it was bigger. It was the night before a happy occasion; this woman couldn't catch a fucking break!

Instead of taking her to the hospital, where she probably would have been admitted, the doctor, aware of the scheduled party, ordered her to go to her office. It was now 9:00 PM. Her doctor had left her personal dinner with her husband to care for my mother on a Saturday night in her office. She hydrated her and prescribed her a stronger anti-seizure medicine. She nursed her back to cognition, and she was on her way. While this was unfolding, I was on standby with my wife and Jessica Crimi, ready to cancel the party and notify the guests.

She woke up the next day refreshed and full of energy. The show must go on. She was surprised and could not stop thanking us for her beautiful day. Mom looked amazing. She pulled it off, and she had the time of her life that day in the presence of the ones closest to her. That would be the last time most of the people in attendance would see her that way.

I'd made the right move; she started to deteriorate after Christmas. It would be the last New Year's Eve I would see her alive. She struggled to make it to Francesca's second birthday at the end of January.

I recall her telling Stephanie that she was happy that she made the holidays and the grandkids' birthdays, and now she could go in peace.

It was now February 7, the day I would take the LSAT, the Law School Admissions test for the entrance into law school. I was more nervous that I had to take the four-hour exam with my cell phone off and that my mother could pass away during that time than actually taking the test.

I raced home after the test to find my mother still alive, in bed. I held her hand, told her I did phenomenally, and I made two commitments to her at her bedside. First, I would write a book about Michael and the eleventh, and second, I would become an attorney one day. She smiled and told me I could do anything I set out to do. Nothing will ever stand in my way of fulfilling my promises to her.

It was now the week of February twentieth. Her condition was worsening. We could not keep up with the pace of the debilitation that was happening right before our eyes. We needed help.

We had hospice care, and a nurse come to help us around the clock. We told Mom everything we had to tell her once again. The pain was enormous. The matriarch, the leader of our family, the woman who instilled the strongest life values in me was dying, fading away right in front of us, and we couldn't do anything.

The suffering became intense. Gasping for air at times, reaching out to me for help tore me apart. She slipped into a coma on February 23, 2009. I would never hear her voice or see her smile ever again. First my brother, now my mother; the people I love the most were now gone forever. How would I get through this?

The afternoon of the twenty-third, while in a coma, the doctor told us the patient can sometimes hear what you say but are unable to respond verbally. I seized the opportunity to thank her once more for being the greatest mother in the world, a true inspiration to me as I venture to achieve greatness. I told her, "I love you, Momma. It's okay to go. You don't have to hang on anymore. We will all be okay. Go and be with Michael. You did your job here. Michael needs you. It is okay to let go, Momma." As I was speaking to her, I heard her sighing, as if she heard every single word I said and acknowledged my request.

That night, I went home to sleep in New Jersey. My sister, Kim, slept in New Jersey as well, and Stephanie and Francesca slept in Staten Island at her parents' house.

I was home in bed alone, tossing and turning; cold sweats and anxiety dominated me. I had a dream about a friend of mine, Kevin Griswold, who had passed away three years earlier. I was at his wake again. I woke at 4:20 AM, when my telephone rang.

With all of her family away and just my father at her bedside, my mother passed away. The suffering for her was now over. She is now with her son and God.

We returned to the house she had been building in Florida with my father. The initial feeling was emptiness; we were walking through the halls of the house in which she had vowed to grow old with my father. I slowly walked over to the fireplace and started to look at all the photos of the family she had strategically placed on the walls to look like bricks. There were pictures of us as a family, theoretically cemented on the wall with strength and longevity. There was also huge portrait of Michael directly over the mantle. What amazed me most about her pictures was how level the picture frames were. She hung them with love and care. I ventured to the left exposure of her gallery to find five empty picture frames that were hung crooked. They filled the void on the wall, but clearly, she couldn't have hung them. And then it hit me. She had been down to the house for the last time about six weeks before her death; she hung these frames, weak with no strength or coordination, because she just wanted to get them up. She knew she would never be there again. She just wanted the frames up, reminding us to fill them with memories after she was gone. We will never level out those frames, but we will honor her unspoken request and fill them with the memories to come in the near future.

My mother had been a great inspiration to me. Sometimes I still find myself dialing her phone number during the day to speak to her. I miss her greatly, but I am at peace with the fact of her death. I had the privilege of having an amazing relationship with her. Her guidance has played an instrumental role in my life success. She will be missed but never forgotten. I love you, Mom. Until we meet again.

Matriarch and Her Family
Notice how my mother has her entire arms wrapped around our family,
as if she was protecting us all.

Chapter 22

In Search of the Sunrise

With all this chaos that rained down in my life over the past few years, I desperately searched for answers to many questions that lurked deep in a shadowy corner in my head. What happened to Mike that day? Who was with him? What did he see? Did he die instantly? Why is my life so different? Why did I live and he die? Will I be able to mend the damaged friendships? Will I ever find these answers, or will I have to deal with the pain of not knowing forever?

I reunited with an old friend from Staten Island, who also was friends with Michael, named Ronn Pearson. Ronn, a few years older than me, someone I truly love, became someone I aspire to be like one day. He is a caring, knowledgeable, mature individual who became a cornerstone in the recovery I had recently undergone in my life. Ronn helped me recognize that the death of Michael, as well as all the trials and tribulations I had been going through, had positive aspects to them. He made it crystal clear to me that what Mike lived for, and what he died for, changed the lives of many and the gift he gave to them he also gave to me. The only thing I had to do was realize the gift and then embrace it. If, and only if I did, would I live a life of happiness again. The gift was the difference in all of our lives he made. A part of him molded me into the person I am today.

Life Coach
Ronn Pearson and me

I consider Ronn Pearson a hero of mine; he helped me when I was at the lowest point of my life. He empowered me to cope with the tragedy and actually look to it from time to time for inspiration to achieve the goals I set out to do. He is responsible for helping me get my emotions in order and played a huge part in helping me gain control of my life again.

Steve Sciarrino, who also played an instrumental role in my rebound, told me, "Joe, did you ever think that your brother died in this life so you can do great things?" Until he pointed that out, I never thought that for a second. It began to make more and more sense as I dwelled on what Steve asked me. From the moment those words came out of his mouth and were received by my ears, the tide began to turn emotionally for me. Mike didn't die in vain. He laid his life down for strangers and fellow firefighter brothers, but most of all, he died for me.

From the second those towers fell and Mike passed on, I began to look at life differently. I did a complete about-face in how I lived. I became driven; I had an uncontrollable thirst for knowledge and a strong desire to lead. I recognized how short life could be and wanted to make the rest of my stay here in the physical as productive as possible. But to do so, I had to regain the support of those who were in my life before all hell broke loose.

It would be systematic and spread over the better part of two years. I reached out to Jerome, Brandon, Chris, and my cousin, each separately via cell phone and e-mail. I wanted to clarify that we all had invested a lot of time in each other's lives, and we did so for a reason, because we loved each other, and to terminate those relationships, some for more than two-thirds of our lives, would be a complete and total shame. Severe damage had been done, but the work I had put in to mend the relationships I had compromised was well worth the effort. Now I have no regrets.

Everything was coming full circle now. The only thing standing the way of my unimpeded path to ultimate happiness once again was closure with Michael's death. The daunting task of trying to reconstruct what the last moments of Mike's life had been like was chiseling away at my soul, until one day when I was working a night tour at Engine 54, Ladder 4 in Midtown.

I was sitting in the firehouse kitchen with some veteran firefighters, trying to retrace the steps of Mike's fire company on the morning of the eleventh. All of a sudden, one of the men told me the men from Engine 54, my company, and Engine 74, Ladder 11 were all on the same floor of building three of the World Trade Center when the collapse of the South Tower took place. He furnished me with a man's number, who was there with my brother. He was firefighter Johnson from Engine 74. Engine 74 had lost one member that day, Ruben Correa; the rest of the company survived. I rushed to call FF Johnson. I will never forget the way my stomach turned as he answered the phone and began to tell me the detailed information I had sought for almost five years. As I braced myself, clutching the phone with all my might, listening as if I didn't want to miss a word, I remember my heart beating so fast and loudly I could barely hear his voice.

He told me Ladder 11 was redirected from operating in the South Tower to operate on the top floor of the Marriott, because one of the airplane's engines had crashed through the top floors of the Marriot and lodged itself on the upper floors, causing fire and heavy smoke conditions. Engines 54 and 74 were teamed up with Ladder 11 doing search and rescue. He remembered Ladder 11 had a probie with them. They were all about to walk down to the floor below when all of a sudden, the sound of a freight train and an immense vibration froze everyone in their tracks. Then it went black, and they were in darkness. Everyone called out to each other, but Rueben Correa from 74 was missing and so were the members of Ladder 11 and Engine 54. Michael was gone. He went on to tell me Mike was standing right next to Rueben when the building collapsed, just ten feet away from the survivors. Two-thirds of the Marriott was sheared off and one-third stood unscathed, and that's where the survivors were. Mike had been ten feet from life, ten lousy, fucking feet. Ten feet meant the difference of being alive or vanishing from this earth forever. The second I heard the news, I wished I'd never searched and discovered it; ten feet meant he almost had a chance. It made me sick.

It took months for me to realize that although the news that he was three yards or so from life might haunt me forever, it was the closure I had hunted for half a decade. I finally knew where he was and what had happened. The wondering, the pain of not knowing, was now gone, and I was one step closer to being my old self.

Now I had answers to many of the questions I had asked over the years. Some may never be answered. I have stopped searching for them. I want him to rest in peace, and I am confident that if I continue to search, he will never rest. I know he is happy that I have reassembled the old relationships he and I had, because they molded us into the men we became. As for Maria, my first wife, I also can positively say that when she asked me, "When is all this 9-11 stuff going to be over, when is it my turn to be happy?" I truly can revisit that question not as being devastating or hurtful, as I first viewed it. She was right. She entered into a marriage just as every woman does, with expectations of living happily ever after. At that time in my life, with the chaos that surrounded us, I couldn't provide that life. I have put any negativity related to her to rest and have since run into her several times; we both wish each other the best.

I think I see a brighter future, a bright light out in the distance. It is my old life, a life filled with happiness.

In life, there is nothing more rewarding to one's soul than gazing out freely into the horizon and being successful in one's search for the sunrise.

The Search
Me looking out to the sunrise in the Keys

Chapter 23

Reflection of Hope

The negative thoughts, stresses, and haunting memories of the eleventh have been recently buried in a shallow grave deep in the catacombs within my mind. Although I will never forget them, I have laid any negativity to rest. I have compartmentalized the memories and have become strong enough to access them in a controlled manner when I desire.

Without question, the events of that day have altered my person, but they did not alter the life I was put here to live. This event will no longer be viewed as a tragedy. To do so would only ensure the longevity of the negativity that once dominated me.

The death of Michael on the eleventh, and the horrific memories of what I saw with my own eyes that day have tempered my soul as if I were a piece of recovered steel from those buildings: one exposed to extreme conditions yet has come out even stronger than when first thrown into the inferno.

Valuable lessons can be learned from what I went through. I hope that my family, friends, or anyone who is exposed to my story or what I have been through can relate to it in some way, shape, or form. Whether someone lost a loved one, their job, or life savings, when your journey through life gets challenging and you think you are defeated, that's the negativity; don't give in to it. Search diligently for a positive way out of the situation. No matter how chaotic or bad it may be, something good is living within; you just have to find it. It is there.

This is the gift that Michael and September 11, 2001, have left me. I have finally identified it.

Although the loss of Michael, all those who were killed, and the ones who still live in grief are disastrous on all fronts, good things have come into my life as a result of the eleventh. I now strive to enjoy all aspects of life, something I didn't do before the eleventh.

September 11, 2001, truly was the day Michael gave his life so I could experience true happiness. He sacrificed his life so my entire family could be blessed with the lives of Stephanie, Francesca, and my niece, Christina Michael. Without his death and the post-traumatic stress that temporarily controlled me, my first marriage to Maria may have worked. Then I wouldn't have met Steph or had Francesca. Christina Michael would not have been here, either. Kim married a firefighter who lost his wife in the World Trade Center. If she had lived, Kim wouldn't have met Ed and conceived Christina.

Mike gave his life so I could become driven, committed, and have the ability to execute my dreams and aspirations.

Before the eleventh, I was not nearly as committed to carrying out my dreams. Today, I am armed with the drive that can strategically overcome any roadblock that stands in my way. As I journey through life and cross paths with many people, this is one of the things I try to instill in them.

Every morning I wake up and get out of bed. I take a slow walk over to the mirror, stare at myself, and look deep within my soul. I must say, I don't see negativity and disaster anymore. I am fortunate enough to see happiness looking back at me. I am blessed to see a vibrant reflection of hope.

Reflection of Hope
This is an actual photo taken by my mother, Linda

"The world ain't all sunshine and rainbows. It's a very mean and nasty place, and I don't care how tough you are, it will beat you to your knees and keep you down permanently if you let it, you, me and nobody is gonna hit as hard as life, but it ain't about how hard you hit, it's about how hard you can get hit, and keep moving forward, how much you can take, and keep moving forward!"- *Rocky- from Balboa 2009*

Please visit the Authors personal website to sign the guestbook, blog, or view in the news updates on the author and his work.

www.911faceofcourage.com

IF

If you can keep your head when all about you
Are losing theirs and blaming it on you,
If you can trust yourself when all men doubt you
But make allowance for their doubting too,
If you can wait and not be tired by waiting,
Or being lied about, don't deal in lies,
Or being hated, don't give way to hating,
And yet don't look too good, nor talk too wise:

If you can dream--and not make dreams your master,
If you can think--and not make thoughts your aim;
If you can meet with Triumph and Disaster
And treat those two impostors just the same;
If you can bear to hear the truth you've spoken
Twisted by knaves to make a trap for fools,
Or watch the things you gave your life to, broken,
And stoop and build 'em up with worn-out tools:

If you can make one heap of all your winnings
And risk it all on one turn of pitch-and-toss,
And lose, and start again at your beginnings
And never breath a word about your loss;
If you can force your heart and nerve and sinew
To serve your turn long after they are gone,
And so hold on when there is nothing in you
Except the Will which says to them: "Hold on!"

If you can talk with crowds and keep your virtue,
Or walk with kings--nor lose the common touch,
If neither foes nor loving friends can hurt you;
If all men count with you, but none too much,
If you can fill the unforgiving minute
With sixty seconds' worth of distance run,
Yours is the Earth and everything that's in it,
And--which is more--you'll be a Man, my son!

--Rudyard Kipling

CPSIA information can be obtained
at www.ICGtesting.com
Printed in the USA
BVHW031738090423
662019BV00012B/129/J